ARRANGING DECK CHAIRS ON THE TITANIC:

Crises in Education

Also by the Author

Fiction:

MUCKALUCK
ON THE RUN
STRAIGHT CUT DITCH

Non Fiction:

ON THE JOB:
  A PRACTICAL GUIDE TO WRITING THAT WORKS
ROBERT COOVER
WILLIAM GOLDMAN

ARRANGING DECK CHAIRS ON THE TITANIC:
Crises in Education

by Richard Andersen

AMANA BOOKS
58 Elliot Street
Brattleboro, Vermont 05301

Copyright © 1988 Amana Books
All rights reserved.

ISBN 0-915597-62-4
ISBN 0-915597-67-5

AMANA BOOKS
58 Elliot Street
Brattleboro, Vermont 05301

Cover Design by: Eric Decker and Kathryn Kraus

Children enter school as question marks
and leave as periods.

                              Neil Postman

FOR THE TEACHERS:

Deborah Shea, Jess Bessinger, Sigfried, Bruce Forer, Bobby Forrest, Patrick Cullen, Mason Cooley, Warren French, Philip Spitzer, Jim Anton, Roni Natov, Vivian Feldman, Bob Greene, George Merolla.

AND THE STUDENTS:

Maura Whelan, Anne Stainback, Mike Badalucco, Andy Rabinowitz, Steve Rosner, Hutch Perry, Lisa Montfort, Ingrid Amble, Aida Estrada.

CONTENTS

Introduction ix

I   Welcome Aboard............................1
    Parents....................................1
    Teachers...................................9
    Students..................................17
    What Happened?...........................18

II   The Lower Decks...........................21
    St. Emeric's School.......................21
    St. Xavier High School....................26
    Alexander Hamilton High School............33
    Sarah J. Hale High School.................36

III   Manning the Pumps........................43
    1. *Eliminate the Bad*......................48
    2. *Improve the Rest*.......................50
    3. *Reward the Good*........................55
    4. *Recruit the Promising*..................58

IV   The Upper Decks...........................66
    1. *Getting Your Papers*....................70
    2. *The Floating Bottom*....................76
    3. *The View from the Bridge*...............81
    4. *Social Activities*......................89
    5. *Three Case Histories*...................94

V   The Tip of the Iceberg...................107

Introduction

I've been wanting to write a book about education for the last twenty years. The kind of book that told people what was really going on in their schools. Two things stopped me: I didn't think the book would sell (people don't buy what they don't want to hear) and I knew no one would believe me.

President Reagan changed my mind. The year was 1985. The Marines hadn't been blown up in Beirut *yet*, the CIA had *yet* to mine Nicaragua's harbor, and the nation's economic recovery was purring along just fine, thank you. Life was quiet in the land of Sam. A little too quiet. The media had nothing with which to keep everyone's anxiety level up. An army of candidates running for the Democratic nomination tried to give them something, but Reagan upstaged them by focusing the public's attention on a subject his opponents had either overlooked or disregarded as unimportant: education. Reagan suggested that teachers compete for merit raises rather than receive regularly scheduled increments in pay.

Teachers associations (predictably) were against the idea. The Democrats (just as predictably) were caught off guard and, by the time they came up with a response, it was too late. The spotlight was back on Reagan, who waited for it in a high school classroom with a copy of *Macbeth* in his hands. Mission accomplished. Case closed. On to another ten-minute attention span.

But not with this viewer. I had seen a lot of deserving teachers get booted out of education because they threatened the mediocre colleagues assigned to evaluate them for merit increases. I knew, given the kind of people who enter the teaching profession, Reagan's idea wasn't nearly as good as it sounded. So I took time out from a novel I was writing – a big mistake if you know anything about writing novels – to voice my opinion in an article. It was only a few pages long, but I was amazed at how easily I said what I had to say. Previously, my writing had always been a struggle. This article seemed effortless by comparison. And instead of being drained by it, I was shaking with rage when I finished.

The only problem was no educational magazine would publish it, which made me realize just how into the *business* of education they are. For them to print my article would be like General Motors coming out and saying, "Okay, you're right. Our cars are lousy; you might as well buy a Datsun."

Then I sent the article to *Time* and *Newsweek* and got some nice comments on it, but by that time the subject was no longer topical. Nobody cared anymore.

But I did. And still do. Which is pretty much how I got started on this book. I'd been teaching off and on for over twenty years. I'd seen a lot and like to think I've learned more than a little. You'll be the best judge of that. All I'm hoping is by the time we're through, you'll never look at a student or a teacher or a school the same way again.

I don't know when I decided to teach or even why. I know it was sometime before the seventh grade. I wasn't very popular, but all the teachers were. Perhaps I wanted to be admired and respected. Even being feared was better than being unknown. If you'd asked me then about teaching, I would have said it was neat. I'd probably still say that.

Whatever my reasons, I didn't prepare very well. Like most teachers, I was a poor student. My combined SAT score in high school was only 800 out of a possible 1600, and not one (not one!) of the seven colleges I applied to would admit me. And we're not talking about Harvard or Yale here either. St. Francis College of Brooklyn turned me down.

Fortunately my mother, who was determined that I have a Catholic education, knew a priest who could get me into Loyola University of Los Angeles on academic probation. I did all right at Loyola. I played on the football team, joined a fraternity that made *Animal House* look like *Plant Life*, married Miss Santa Monica, and like most teachers, graduated from the bottom of my class. In my major field of study, English, I got eleven C's and an A.

The A was a gift. Dr. Frank Sullivan, who assigned no books, required no essays, and gave no exams in *Modern Drama*, awarded everyone he knew an A. Attendance, which was never taken, was the only assignment. I saw *Top Hat*, *Shane*, and *Forbidden Planet* before I stopped going. Dr. Sullivan never had a chance to meet me, but he knew my wife. She was a secretary in the English Department. She asked him to give me an A, and he did.

I never took any education courses at Loyola. I didn't even know they existed. But it didn't matter. To teach at St. Emeric's School in New York, you didn't need any education courses. You didn't even need a college degree. All you had to be was desperate, which is why, at the age of twenty-one, with no teaching experience of any kind, I was named Chairman of the English Department. My salary, after taxes came to $315 a month which, after rent and utilities, left me with $15 to spread over thirty days. If my wife hadn't been working, I don't know what I would have done. Probably the same thing I did six years later when I was divorced and taking home *$215* a month as a New York University graduate assistant. I would have stolen all my food, jumped every turnstile that stood in my way, and made whatever money I could posing for pornographic novel covers—the only job to give me decent money *and* the time I needed to teach and study.

When this book ends, I'm the James Thurber writer-in-residence at Ohio State University, but how I got from the streets of Brooklyn to live in the house where the bed fell on father is not so much a success story as that of a person pushed upward because he wasn't allowed to stay on the bottom. By the time we're through, we'll all have learned something from the experience and—if action really is true measurement of a good book—do something about it.

I
Welcome Aboard

Parents

Believe it or not, parents are the single most important force in any school. Teachers and administrators act differently whenever they're around. Unfortunately, few parents know this or, if they do, don't care to exercise their power.

One exception is Mel and Norma Gabler. Mel and Norma were sitting around the kitchen table one night when their son, Jim, told them about a history book that said the federal government has absolute authority over the states. Well that wasn't what Mel and Norma had been taught, so they asked to see their son's book.

The Gablers were stunned. Similar horrors leapt out at them from other pages. And not just factual mistakes. There were moral errors too. Non-smoking, non-drinking members of the fundamentalist Christian Missionary Alliance, the Gablers realized God was calling on them through their son's history book to correct misinformation and restore traditional values to the classroom.

But how were they going to do this? Jim's teachers claimed they didn't choose the books; the state textbook committee did. And when the Gablers first appeared before the committee in 1961, they weren't taken seriously. Local newspapers dubbed Norma the "Dirty Book Lady."

The Gablers wouldn't give up, however. Quitting their jobs to devote every minute they could spare to the cause, they began alerting anyone who would listen to the biased, unpatriotic, and morally permissive lessons that were being taught in our children's schools. What they found shocked parents in every state. One history book, for example, contained an entire chapter on Marilyn Monroe without once mentioning Lyndon Baines Johnson. Another omitted the whole War of 1812.

Today, the Gablers' newsletter reaches 13,000 subscribers, and the couple spends as many as 200 days a year speaking to various religious and civic organizations. They've appeared on 60 Minutes and Donahue, debated with William Buckley, and brought more than one textbook committee around to their way of thinking. Of fifteen books the Gablers recently cited for offenses ranging from graphic sexual instruction to slighting the NASA space program, educators in Texas rejected eleven of them. Moreover, few publishers will even consider going to press with their textbooks before the Gablers have had a look at them. Says Norma: "I've won my right to be heard and I'm not laughed at anymore."

Whether you agree with the Texas Senate, which commended the Gablers, or the American Library Association, which condemmed them as self-appointed censors, the point is the same: parents who care can have a much greater influence on their children's education than they think.

Unfortunately, most parents are too willing to let the schools be responsible for their children's education. I've met a lot of parents over the past twenty years and, with few exceptions, they all have one thing in common: Their children were the best students in my classes. The parents I most needed to see—the ones whose children were in the middle or lower ranks rarely showed up on Parents' Day. And when I ran into them on the street with their sons or daughters and asked how their children were doing in school, they never knew.

In my first three years as a teacher, I worked in two Catholoic schools: a parochial grammar school and a private high school. If I had 125 students each year, I could count on seeing only the parents of the top fifteen or twenty. And though I enjoyed telling these people what a good job they were doing—which was what they had come to hear—it frustrated me to think of all the parents who weren't there.

In my fourth year of teching, I worked in a public high school. Of the 150 students I taught, how many of their parents whould you guess showed up over two Parent's Days? One.

Hard to believe, but true. And the one I met didn't even have a child in my class. Having made the round of her daughter's teachers, this good samaritan decided to stop in on those who didn't have any parents and cheer them up.

Several conclusions may be drawn from these experiences: parents who care send their children to better schools, the best students come from homes where parents take an interest in their education, and private schools are better than public ones.

All wrong. Or at least not all necessarily right. The father of the best private school student I ever had, and himself an educator, once told me, "If Ray ever gives you any trouble, you have my permission to clobber him."

A caring parent if there ever was one, but would you want him teaching your child? Many parents would, which is one reason why you never hear much about physical punishement in the schools until someone is severely injured. Even then you may not know. I saw a kid get three teeth loosened and his parents, not wanting to jeopardize their son's education by taking him out of the school, settled for the principal's promise to cover the orthodontic bills. Nothing more was done about it. Ray's father, a junior high school principal told me how he broke a disobedient child's arm: "I did it in my office with the door closed. No witnesses. It was his word against mine. If he said anything, I would've said he broke it on the way home from school and was blaming it on me, but I never heard a word from anybody."

When I first started teaching, I rarely met a parent I liked. Maybe it was the schools I taught in, but imagine warming up to someone who introduces herself as Mrs. Dr. Rabinowitz or to a father who tells his daughter she doesn't have to participate in the Christmas Grab Bag if she draws the only black person in the class. After most Parents' Days, I used to feel so sorry for some of my students, I wanted to give them all high marks just to offset what it must be like living with Mrs. Dr. Rabinowitz and Co.

Lately, perhaps because I've grown older, the reverse has been true. Most of the parents I meet seem like decent, hard-working people who care very much about their children and are making tremendous sacrifices to send them to the best schools they can afford. Few kids, on the other hand, can appreciate the fact that their education is often the most expensive investment their parents will make after a home.

So where's the middle ground? I'm not always sure. I don't have children and couldn't afford to send them to a good school if I did. In fact, I've only had one experience with teachers that was anything like a concerned parent might face. It took place in Oregon. I was visiting my family when my sister, an English major at Portland State University, showed me the syllabi from her three upper-division courses.

The first covered the entire history of the English novel in three books: *Wuthering Heights*, *Little Dorrit*, and *North and South*.

The second was a course in comedy. Five works were assigned: three movies to be shown in class—though the student was expected to read the books they were adapted from (ho-ho)—*The World According to Garp*, which would open at their local movie theatres before the course was over, and the "Doonesbury" comic strip. Anyone who wanted extra credit could earn it by seeing the movie *Arthur*.

A brief aside: I don't have anything against extra credit. Some students need all they can get, but I think in this case they could've at least written a review of the film. What really bothers me, however, is when a teacher spends hours behind a projector that could be put to better use in front of a blackboard. This teacher had to work in only two-thirds of his classes. And so did his students, which is the very reason why Kathy took the course. It's all part of the unwritten conspiracy that exists between students and teachers and covers everything from assignments and grades to just about anything you can imagine. Basically, the message reads: Let's all do as little as possible and be rewarded for it in the end. If you're a student, this means high grades; if you're a teacher, it means no trouble in class and high marks on your students' evaluation forms.

Back to Portland State. I don't remember Kathy's third English class, but I do remember that not one of the three contained a single essay assignment.

Think about that.

Three upper-division courses, all intended for English majors at a time when SAT scores are going down and businesses all over the country are screaming that students coming out of college today don't know how to write.

Not one single essay assignment.

The day before the English novel take-home final was due, I pulled a Norma Gabler. Kathy wanted to know if I would help her. I said, "sure."

The question, taken almost word for word from a chapter in Dorothy Van Ghent's *The English Novel*, was on *Wuthering Heights*. Kathy hadn't heard of Van Ghent's book. A standard for English majors studying the English novel, but she had read *Wuthering Heights* in high school.

Why not at Portland State?

She thought she'd remember it.

Well why not answer the question on *Little Dorrit* or *North and South*?

She hadn't read them because everyone knows Professor Believe-Me-If-I-Remembered-His-Name-I'd-Print-It only asks one question for each book assigned and, since you only have to answer one question on the exam, you only have to read one book. He's been doing it that way for years.

"So you didn't read any books?"

"I read *Wuthering Heights*."

"I know. In high school."

Two hours later, my mother wants to know why I won't help Kathy with her exam.

I explain the difference between helping Kathy and taking the exam for her.

My mother argues that the exam isn't that important. What counts most is that Kathy gets a degree so she can get a good job. (Kathy, by the way, is in her sixth year of college and has yet to declare her major.)

I wanted to know who's going to do Kathy's work for her once she gets a job, but I don't get an answer. Instead, I hear everything from "Just this time" to what I don't have the strength to refuse: "Do it for me."

Now that may not seem like much of an argument, but if you know someone who set fire to her living room to collect enough insurance money to pay for your last semester in college, you'll understand why I: (1) get into the car. (2) drive to Portland State, (3) buy a copy of *The English Novel*, (4) open it to the chapter on *Wuthering Heights*, and 5) hand it to Kathy, who's watching *General Hospital*.

Then I get on the phone. If Kathy's going to be irresponsible and her own mother is going to help her, perhaps the Chairman of the English Department, the Dean of the College of Liberal Arts, and the President of the university might do something about shoring up their end.

The departmental secretary says she'll see if the chairman is in. "*Whom* may I say is calling?"

"The *father* of one of his students."

"Students" is barely out of my mouth when I hear, "Sorry to keep you waiting," and the secretary is told to disconnect her line. "Which student?" asks the chairman.

I refuse to tell him. "If my daughter knew I was calling her teacher, she'd never forgive me."

"Well I don't see how I can help you if I don't know who your daughter is."

"I'm not calling about my daughter."

"Oh?"

"I'm calling about her professors. Did you know that there are at least 3 courses being offered in your department that don't contain a single essay assignment?

He didn't know. He was new. This was his first year in the school.

"Well now that you know, what are you going to do about it?"

"What are the classes?"

I tell him.

He says he'll get back to me. Three days go by without a word. I call the Dean and tell him what happened. Five

WELCOME ABOARD

minutes after we hang up, the phone rings. It's the chairman. "That wasn't a very nice thing you just did," he says.

"Did you talk to my daughter's teachers?"

"Yes I did."

"And?"

"There's a very good reason why those professors elected not to assign any essays: They're trying to cut down on plagiarism."

Think about that one for a minute. The logic of it. If the students don't write essays, they'll stop plagiarizing. Imagine the extent to which this kind of reasoning can take you. If people stopped driving cars, there wouldn't be any traffic accidents. If chairmen didn't wake up, they'd sleep forever.

The chairman accuses me of insulting him.

I tell him expecting me to believe that nonsense about avoiding plagiarism is an insult.

He hangs up.

I call the Dean.

Five minutes later, the chairman's back on the phone. He's sorry. He's new. He's a little tense.

I ask him if he thinks fear of plagiarism is worth not assigning any essays at all. "What's the difference between that and not reading any books because you don't like unhappy endings?"

"There's a big difference. For one thing, writing is not the same as reading. You can't plagiarize reading."

I can't argue with that one, so I tell him, "If my daughter plagiarized a paper, I'd be happy she opened a book."

He thinks that's funny. He relaxes. We're going to get along now.

"If your professors are so worried about plagiarism, why do they give take-home exams?"

"Because the amount of time given for an exam is shorter than for a paper, usually less than a week."

"That's plenty of time for students who only have to read one book because their professor gives the same kind of exam every semester."

"Are you by any chance a teacher?"

"Yes I am."

"I'll get back to you."

Twenty four hours later, he tells me the professor teaching the English Novel didn't realize the students had detected a pattern in his exams and thanks me for bringing it to the department's attention.

"And what about no essays in the comedy course?"

Another twenty-four hours pass. "If you had read the syllabus instead of listening to your daughter, you'd have seen that the professor is taking a 'non-literary' approach to the subject. He'd be happy to discuss this with you if you wish."

"All I wish is for my daughter to write an essay."

"Her take-home exam is an essay."

I see a big circle looming on the horizon so I get off the phone, count to ten, and call the President of Portland State. I tell him I'm from *Time* magazine and we're doing a feature on why kids today can't write. Is PSU doing anything about it?

"You bet it is."

"What?"

"For one thing, we've insisted on all our professors assigning at least one essay in every course they teach and, for another, we're encouraging the professors to substitute essay exams for multiple choice tests whenever possible."

I tell him what's going on in his own English Department.

He can't believe it. It was the English Department that insisted essay assignments be made an important part of every course.

I say I'll call him in a couple of days. When I do, he isn't in. Every day for a week he's at a meeting or "In conference." Unable to stay in Portland any longer, I return to New York. One month later, Kathy gets her grades. Those in English read: D.
      D.
      D.

My mother is furious. I've ruined everything. Kathy will never graduate now. What did it matter if she didn't read *Wuthering Heights*? Was that any reason to ruin her whole life?

"Mom, I never told them her name."

"They looked it up. She was the only person with that name

in all three classes."

I should have known. Instead of dealing with the problem of the essays, the professors punished Kathy for having a concerned parent. Not that she didn't deserve those grades, but she wasn't given them for the right reasons.

I told my mother—Kathy was no longer speaking to me—to petition for a review. "Have Kathy say she doesn't know what her father said but he wasn't in a position to know, that he's been having trouble at work and taking it out on everybody in the family, and that she'll do any extra work they consider necessary to raise the grades."

More work for Kathy (read: more work for the professors) wasn't necessary. Kathy's final grades? B.
B.
B.

Teachers

The great majority of teachers I've known are either cowards or failures or both. What saves many of them from exposure is a remarkable ability to get rid of anyone who threatens their own mediocrity.

To understand this better, it's necessary to take a look at what kind of people enter the teaching profession. More often than not, they are from the lower ranks of their graduating classes. While our high schools' best students go on to colleges that help them enter more lucrative fields, those who continue their education from the lower end of the scale make up a frighteningly high percentage of the students studying to be teachers. Substituting one night for an exhausted professor at Medgar Evers College in Brooklyn, I met a class of thirty-two women who wanted to teach. Not one of them had scored higher than a third-grade level on a reading assessment exam, and I was supposed to teach them how to correct essays. But because none of them understood what a noun or pronoun was, we spent most of the class finding the "who's" and the "what's" in the exercise of sentences.

Perhaps this is one reason why education classes are the most flyweight in any university. And God help the professor who doesn't keep them that way. I once sat in on an opening class at Columbia University's Teachers College and saw half the students walk out of the room when they heard there was an essay assignment.

In what other field can a person earn a doctorate without having to write a dissertation?

When I was teaching at Boston University's College of Basic Studies — a sort of reform school for rich kids who could enter the university's regular degree programs if they mastered certain basic skills other than math — the poorest students were encouraged to enter the School of Education. It was the easiest major, it kept money coming into the university, and it underscored George Bernard Shaw's famous dictum: "Those who can't do, teach."

The results are predictable: Graduates from the School of Education score well below the average of those from Boston University's other schools. In fact, they score lower in English than the majors in almost every other field.

Nor does the Northeast have a corner on the underachievement market. Several colleges in California can't get more than 60% of their graduating classes to pass the state competency exam, and Portland State University recently graduated an honors student who turned out to be functionally illiterate. During the last teachers' strike in Chicago, one demonstrator told a television reporter, "I teaches English," and *Time* magazine published this note sent by a teacher from Alabama to the parents of one of her students: "Scott want pass in his assignment at all, he had a poem to learn and he fell to do it."

Although these may seem like extreme examples, they are much closer to the norm than many people realize. Teachers such as the one from Alabama don't always stand out, however, because they've found ways to protect themselves — like making their handwriting illegible or relying on the telephone.

One way of eliminating this kind of incompetence is through examinations. Unfortunately, and for obvious reasons, most teachers resent being tested even when the exams aren't that difficult. In Florida's Pinellas County, for example, the school board requires its teacher candidates to have a tenth grade reading level and be able to solve math problems at an eighth grade level. Though all the candidates to take the exam in 1979 held at least a Bachelor's degree, over 25% of them failed.

The National Education Association, predictably, has fought to discredit competency testing on the grounds that teacher competency can't be measured in written tests. While this may be true, it is equally true that testing can weed out some of the incompetents.

The American Federation of Teachers is also against examining teachers, but its members agree that it's a good idea to test *new* candidates, thereby protecting all the incompetents already in the system. If recent studies are accurate, at least 20% of the teachers working in schools today have not mastered the basic skills in reading, writing, and arithmetic that they are supposed to teach. Here are some excerpts from a memo written by a current high-school principal:

> It is a decision of this office to cancel the Thursday's meeting . . . I can no longer tolerate nor accept politically, incline of vested self interest to over-rule our purpose of being.
>
> The school is *not* in trouble. Nor is teachers destined for the bread line. And if anyone seeks to select and enforce this type approach to create further distraction or unrest in the classroom shall be dealt with overtly deliberate and severe.

And don't think incompetence is limited to the elementary and secondary schools. One of my all-time least favorite teachers, a Dean of Faculty at the City University of New York, was famous for reading to his students from the introductions to the books he'd assigned. What would have been painfully boring, however, was made almost entertaining by his inability to keep his place on the page and his butchering of some fairly common words: "epi-tome" for "e-pit-o-me," for example, or "kway" for "quay." Years later, when I ran into him at a conference in Oslo, I told him some of the things I didn't have the courage to say when I was in his class. And his reply? "I was just making sure you were paying attention." Very funny if you've never heard it before, but a stock response to those in the profession and every bit as unimaginative as their classes. A good example of the experienced incompetent's ability to rationalize, it's practically unassailable as a pedagogical device. Every time you catch him on it, he's proven that it works. Unfortunately, I remember the mistakes he made more than anything he ever read about Mark Twain.

Students don't often complain about their teachers' incompetency because they're afraid of having their grades affected, but they can come up with some amusing responses. Early in my career, a department chairman observed (correctly) that I knew very little about how a class should be run and suggested I sit in on his Senior Honors section the following day. He was going to lecture on Albert Camus' *The Stranger*.

I hadn't read the book since high school, which says something about how fast curricula change, so I was looking forward to learning as much about Camus as about teaching when I took an empty seat in the middle of the room.

Mr. Chaffey, a man too insecure in his first year as department chairman to let subordinates call him by his first name, had the names of the book, the author, and the characters he was going to discuss written on the blackboard before class began. His lecture was uninspired, but it seemed to be having a strange effect on the students, who exchanged knowing glances every time Mr. Chaffey answered one of their questions. Some of them looked knowingly at me too, but I had no idea what they were trying to convey until one of the students told Mr. Chaffey that he understood Camus' existential statement as it was presented in *The Stranger* but was confused by the author's apparent reversal in *The Unknown Self*.

Mr. Chaffey explained how Camus' philosophy may have

taken on slightly different variations over the course of his career, but his central existential perspective was constant in every book he wrote.

This made sense to me, but the students could barely stifle their laughter. While I looked around the room for some clue to what was going on, someone slipped a note on to my desk. It read, "Camus never wrote a book called *The Unknown Self*."

The whole class had been making a fool of Mr. Chaffey or, perhaps more accurately, helping him make a fool of himself. Which is a good lesson in not being afraid to admit when you don't know something. In fact, the students will respect you more for being honest and human, and they'll appreciate whatever effort you make to find an answer. You might even ask the class to join you in finding out what all of you need to know. Now that may seem obviously sensible to most people, but, to an insecure teacher, the idea of admitting ignorance can be terrifying.

What makes this story exceptional, however, is the intelligence of these particular students. Most kids would have used a title like *The Friend* or *Stranger No More*. I never would have even *thought* of the idea. While the high schoolers of my generation were putting tacks on each other's chairs or gluing the pages of the class egghead's books together, I was taught and I *believed* that Cochise was a graduate of Harvard, that the Grand Canyon contains every natural color in the world, that physical punishment is a sign of love, and that grass is the second most powerful force in nature (after tidal waves) because it can push its way through concrete. Intellectually insecure teachers such as Mr. Chaffey had nothing to fear from us.

Who, then, are they afraid of? Not administrators. As long as teachers can keep their students in their seats, get their grades in on time, and not have any pictures of spring on the bulletin board when the superintendent visits in January, they won't be troubled. And not the parents either. They're the last to want to know if their children aren't getting a good education. And if they did find out, what alternatives would they have? They couldn't get rid of all the incompetent teachers without causing chaos, and many parents couldn't afford to send their children to better schools. It's better *not* to know what's going on.

So who are the teachers afraid of? You wouldn't be far off the mark if you said, "Themselves," but, given the generally unreflective nature of the profession, "Other teachers" might be more accurate. In other words, now you know why so many of your favorite instructors never lasted very long. They made the others look bad. Bright, ambitious, able to stimulate their students, they threatened the status quo by exposing the mediocrity in it. How could they, a few idealists who possibly rejected the prosperity of another profession because they wanted to do something meaningful with their lives, compete against an entrenched army whose members started out as middlers in school, entered a profession they knew was easy, and continued following the path of least resistance by never varying their syllabi or becoming administrators? If I told you the number of teachers who told me that as long as their schools were going to pay them to do nothing they might as well stay, you wouldn't believe me. If I told you the number of administrators I know who have made teaching their second jobs, you'd say I was making it up.

Jim Anton was not of this mold. He may have been incompetent and a trouble-maker to his department chairman and the assistant principal, but to me and not a few others he was one of those rare individuals able to produce that enviable blend of care, energy, learning, and imagination that good teaching requires.

Ironically, he wasn't a teacher. Or at least he didn't plan to be. But like a lot of people trying to beat the draft and Viet Nam, he wound up in the classroom. Considering how many people postponed more promising careers by teaching during that terrible time, it could have been a high-water mark for the profession if so many of the radical ideas they brought with them had been better tested or more carefully thought out. Unlike a lot of teachers, however, who used their views as an excuse to avoid detailed schoolwork, Jim combined them with his own sense of discipline. He may have thought competition was immoral, grades undemocratic, and promotion based on merit discriminatory towards minorities and the poor, but he also knew the backward thinking of people who believed children had to feel good about themselves before they could learn. When students learned, they felt good about themselves.

A published poet as well as a scientist, Jim wasn't afraid to risk failure in trying something new. I remember walking by his class one day; the whole room was buzzing. Jim had just finished a lesson on aerodynamics and was challenging his students to see how many workable paper airplanes they could design. The reasons for their success or failure were to be written in a homework assignment. Before the class was over, the students came up with eleven imaginative designs to keep paper in the air, but anyone walking by would have thought the class had gotten out of control. At least that's what Jim's chairman told the assistant principal.

Few people contrasted more sharply with Jim Anton than his chairman, a Russian immigrant who memorized clichès to improve his English. Unfortunately, Chairman Gabor couldn't keep the clichès straight and was always saying things like "I went over that material with a fine toothpick" or "When I walk into a room, those kids don't say 'mum'." He wasn't much better at science either, having told one class that a light year was about three minutes long.

The assistant principal, however, made Jim's chairman look like a genius. The teachers called him "Napoleon's Lieutenant" after a story about how Napoleon always chose for his first lieutenant the dumbest man in France. The nation's biggest idiot could understand his general's orders, there was no reason for anyone else not to.

Jim didn't have a chance. I think the final blow came when the assistant principal heard music coming from the science lab. Jim's students had just finished building their own radio, but their teacher was reprimanded for letting them listen to rock-n-roll.

Just firing Jim Anton would have been bad enough, but the chairman and the assistant principal tried to discredit him as well by yelling at him in front of his students for talking during a fire drill and not letting him chaperone a school dance because he hadn't worn a tie. They also harassed him by assigning him more substitution periods than anyone else and making sure he had no "personal papers" on him whenever he used the school's photocopy machine.

It must be admitted, however, that Jim didn't help matters any when, remembering his chairman's definition of a light year, he listed the size of his lab jacket as an hour and a half.

The other teachers didn't like what was going on but felt powerless to do anything. They didn't belong to any union and couldn't expect the principal to overrule two of his appointees in favor of an untenured faculty member.

So they held a meeting. Of the school's sixty teachers, about half religious and half laymen, eighteen showed up. None had taken a vow of obedience. After much discussion, it was decided that Richard, an English teacher who had discovered his own chairman correcting papers while his students watched "Rocky and Bullwinkle" on television, should write a letter asking the administration to remember the Christian values on which the school was founded.

Richard wrote the letter, signed his name, tacked it onto the faculty bulletin board, and went off to class imagining the rush of people to add their signatures.

Only one person signed.

ONE PERSON!

And he wasn't even at the meeting!

Three nights later, Jim's best friend showed up at Richard's door. Mike had been drinking since the letter went up and felt awful. A night of confessions ranging from sexual impotency to failure to be a doctor followed, but the next day there were two signatures on the letter.

But it was too late. The letter had needed signatures right away to demonstrate the intensity of the faculty's concern. By the end of the week, knowing no harm could come to the second person on the list, four more teachers added their names.

So Jim was fired and so was Richard. Today, they're both grateful for the push. Basically cowards who would have stayed had they been allowed to, they can look back at the bored, alienated state of many of their former colleagues and know the administration was right: They didn't belong.

WELCOME ABOARD

Students

A lot has been written about students: How in 1900 when only 6% of American children graduated from high school, they looked up to their teachers as scholars; how the decline of the family and increase in working mothers have eroded the students' respect for authority; how television has reduced their attention span to the time between commercial breaks; how busing, Viet Nam, Watergate, the Me Culture, the increase in violence (up 57% from 1978), and the national policy of keeping students in school regardless of their aptitude or attitude have distracted them from their studies; how such faddish theories as the New Math, the "open classroom," and the "look-say" approach to reading (as opposed to learning to read by sounding out syllables) have caused more confusion than anything else; and finally, how so many of our culture's heroes are so blatantly undereducated, which is not to say they aren't bright, just that they give very little evidence of having been to a school.

To this list can be added the prevalent conspiracy between teachers and students to do as little work as possible.

The teacher-student conspiracy is mostly a result of "teacher burn-out." Teacher burn-out occurs most frequently in the poorer schools, which have the most difficult students and consistently receive the youngest and most untried teachers, but it's also common among university professors who have worked night and day to achieve high evaluations from their students, serve on as many committees as possible, and publish as much as they can only to collapse into inertia once they're awarded tenure.

The burn-outs are easy to recognize. They're the ones who ask their students to show how many did their homework by raising their hands. They're the ones who take all their sick days because they can't stand to be in the classroom anymore. They're the ones who assign the same books, essays, and exams year after year. They're the ones that don't require homework because "the kids can't read." They're the ones who sleep through their preparation periods, feel they can't compete with television, and acclaim as "outstanding" and "excellent" papers containing dozens of uncorrected mistakes.

Here's one telling description of teacher burn-out and its effects. It was written by Aida Estrada, a twenty-six-year-old student from Manhattan Community College:

What Happened?

Miss Castel was my home room teacher in junior high school. There she also teached English.

Miss Castel was not a tall women. But she had the most prettyest blue eyes and blue hair I ever seen.

But she was always anger. I never new why she was so anger. I always though she was not happy doing what she was doing has a teacher.

But all and all Miss Castel and me got along very well. One day Miss Castel asked me if I would like to be in her English Class. Of course I said yes.

After I graduate junior high school I went on to high school.

There I had Miss Castel for my English class again. And again there all I learned was checker and chess.

She never teached me any thing about writing or reading English the right way. Again I pasted with an A+.

That next year I made sure that I was not going to be in her class again.

I really don't know what happen to her. She at one time was the best English teacher there could be.

I don't know what her problem could have been. But checker was not the best thing to teach student.

I mean I do like checker and chess but not every day. I would have like to learn some thing. So that now I wouldn't have to be taking a remedial class in English in college. It not that I don't enjoy my English teacher now the way he teaches but imagine for two years take English in Checker.

In other words, teacher burn-outs are the ones who have given up and are too depressed to do anything more about it than make life easy on their students in the hope they'll reciprocate.

Ironically, most of the students only make it harder. What do they care if their teachers are defeated and depressed. They're boring! And when the students are bored, watch out. They don't sit in their seats, read from their books, or pay attention in class. Instead—at least at the lower levels—they talk continuously, get into fights, throw spitballs, steal schoolbags, eat erasers, make endless trips to the bathroom, and think of countless ways to entertain themselves by making their teachers' lives miserable. As a student, I remember stuffing one teacher's lectern with marbles and an alarm clock set to go off fifteen minutes into the class, filling the seat of another's chair with water, mouthing words so that a third would think his hearing aid was broken, and in unison with thirty others, tearing a piece of paper out of my spiral notebook at 10 a.m., crumpling it into a ball at 10:05, and throwing it into a wastepaper basket at 10:10.

The upper levels of high school and college are different, though similar pranks have been known to take place. By that time, however, the students have usually grown up a bit. They've entered a world where their position isn't much different from that of teachers in the sense that the less work they have to do the more time they have to watch television and hang out with their friends.

So they play the game. They don't bother teachers who'll give them time to do their homework in class or object to teachers who'll spend the better part of an hour discussing an upcoming game with the class jocks. They'll also show an interest in their teachers' anecdotes, laugh at their jokes, and come up with an endless supply of questions that have absolutely nothing to do with the subject they're supposed to be studying.

But they expect more in return than free time or distractions. They want high grades as well. Warning: Parents, beware of high marks in any classes for which your child does little homework. Students today receive 25% more A's and B's than they did fifteen years ago, but many of them have to be taught how to fill out a job application. Over the past ten years, student achievement levels have dropped consistently in reading, writing, science, social studies, and mathematics.

When I taught my first senior class in high school, thirty students came into the room, sat down, and stared at me through the most vacuous collection of eyes I'd ever seen. And they stayed that way for eight months. Nothing I did—not even tap dancing my way through a poem to demonstrate the beat—could move them. Like so many prisoners, they were doing their time, counting the days to the weekend, the next vacation, or whatever else would free them. Finally, around the beginning of April, they started to come alive, but by that time I was dead, the frustration of no response having taken the life out of me long ago. Now it was I who couldn't wait to be free from students who'd been taught they would be rewarded for not causing any trouble.

Whatever can be said about students, however, one truth always holds: if there is any satisfaction in teaching, they are where it is found. If they are the reason we entered the profession, they will be the ones to see us through it. No matter how deficient they become, they are the teachers' only salvation. Nobody else—not parents, administrators, or colleagues—can provide that special recognition which comes when a student learns something. You may not be aware of it until many years later, when a long forgotten but quickly remembered face shows up to tell you, but when it happens, there's nothing like it. It makes all the frustration, pain and exhaustion worthwhile.

II

The Lower Decks

St. Emeric's School

St. Emeric's School separates a white, middle-class housing project and a mostly Puerto Rican *barrio*. The teachers are Irish or Sisters of Charity or both. The school play, more often than not, is *Finnegan's Rainbow*. Get the picture?

I didn't. I was twenty-one years old, just out of college, and Sister Muriel was the only principal who would hire me. She told me the money wasn't much ($5,000 a year), but at least I'd be able to tell people I was Chairman of an English Department. No one had to know I was its only member.

As Chairman, my responsibilities included cleaning my classroom, monitoring the cafeteria, forming an intramural sports league, teaching a religion I didn't believe in, and driving one of the sisters to her mother's house on the first and last Thursday of every month. The tough part was coming up with a list of books the students would enjoy and I didn't have to re-read. *Romeo and Juliet*, *Gulliver's Travels*, *Huckleberry Finn*, and *The Scarlet Letter* were the only ones I could remember reading in college. I knew they were too advanced for most eleven and twelve year olds, but what could I do? The first day of class was less than forty-eight hours away, when she saw my reading list.

Sister Muriel wondered if I might be robbing the children of the joy of reading these works for the first time in high school.

Had I known what I know now, I would have said the children were never even going to *hear* of these books in high school, but I told her I was giving the students a head start. The truth was I had absolutely no idea what else to assign them and didn't have any time to find one.

Sister Katherine, the head of the Math Department, told me not to worry about it. The important thing was that the children read. Even a comic book could improve their skills.

This struck me as very profound. I was once a voracious reader of comic books, especially the old *Classics Illustrated*. I read some of them more than a hundred times. When I got to high school, I translated Caesar's *Gallic Wars* almost solely on what I remembered from the comic book (Father Lelesy could never figure out how I managed to translate some passages so well and others so poorly), and later, when I was in graduate school, I used what I remembered from the *Classics Illustrated* version of *The Red Badge of Courage* on my doctoral comprehensives. Even now, the cartoon of Jim Conklin's death is more real to me than the scene Crane portrayed. Unfortunately, my mother, thinking I was too old for comic books, threw them all out when I was twelve. I didn't read anything for years after that, not even the newspaper. I still don't read much more than I have to.

So based on my limited experience, Sister Katherine's simplistic statement made a lot of sense. Others followed, and in every one, she seemed so on top of things, so sure of herself. Like the time she told me not to smile until Christmas. I thought that was a brilliant way of saying you could always loosen up on the students but you couldn't always tighten up on them.

"On the first day of class," said Sister Katherine, "I stand by the door and give each child a stern look in the eye as they enter the room. They know they can leave their monkey business out in the hall. And I don't let them sit down either. They have to stand against the back wall while I assign their seats individually. I tell them I've made a record of all the marks on all the desks and they'd better be in the same condition in June as they are in September. I've got better things to do with my time than sand desks."

I followed Sister Katherine's advice and it worked like a charm. As Chairman Gabor would say, those kids didn't say "mum." But what would I do about the second day? And the third?

Sister Katherine told me not to worry. "The Irish kids won't give you any trouble. They're reasonable. Their parents have been telling them since they were babies what's right and what's wrong. All you have to do is talk to them and they'll understand. With the Puerto Ricans and blacks, it's different. They don't listen to reason. At home, their parents beat them if they misbehave. It's the only thing they understand and, unfortunately, the only thing they respect. So don't be afraid to cuff one of them on the back of the head if you feel you have to."

That didn't seem very sound to me, but what did I know? Sister Katherine had been right all along, and sure enough, she was right again. The white kids all did what they were told, while the blacks and Puerto Ricans couldn't sit still for more than five minutes at a time. And no sooner did I get one settled down than three more started talking to their friends, jumping out of their seats, and wanting to go to the bathroom.

I didn't know when I hit that first child. I don't even remember what he did. But whatever it was, I'll never forget the look in his eyes. They said, "I can't hit you back because you're bigger than me, but I just got the better of you."

Flashback: Brooklyn, New York, 1958. Things had gone from bad to worse since the Dodgers left. Now we'd been separated from the girls, who'd been taught by the nuns while Franciscan Brothers took care of us. All last year we heard what the Franciscans weren't going to let us get away with.

I don't remember whether Brother Neri had us line up against the back wall, but he did make us stand next to our desks while he walked up and down the aisles slapping each one of us into his seat. "And that's the least anyone who busts my chops can expect," he announced when he was through.

Brother Neri's chops will never be the same. We must have broken them four or five times a day. The first time I broke them was when I couldn't spell the word "principal." Sounding it out like the nuns had taught us, I spelled, "P-r-i-n-c-e-i-p-a-l."

"Spell it again."
"P-r-i-n-c-e-i-p-a-l."
"Come up here."
I went up to Brother Neri's desk.
"Now spell "principal."
"Prince. P-r-i-n-c-e--"

I was concentrating so hard on the word, I never knew what hit me. And it all happened so fast, I wasn't even hurt. That was the amazing part. I had been knocked over a student's desk and thrown on the floor and I didn't even feel it. "P-r-i-n-c-i-p-a-l," I heard myself say while still on my back.

"There, you see!" said Brother Neri. "I knocked it into you."

Into me or out of me, Brother Barnabas, our eighth-grade teacher, made Brother Neri look like a creampuff. If you missed more than three spelling words on one of Brother Barnabas's daily quizzes, you never missed more than three words again. The crack of what he called his "board of education" on your hand was so loud, teachers on the floor below had to shut their doors. I still don't have to close my eyes to see Eddie MacDonald's hands bleeding on the day he only got three right.

The hitting fell off in high school, but I can remember Father Lelesy punching Joe Latter in the face because he was leaving school without his Latin book (Joe claimed he'd done his homework during a study period), and Brother Vincent loosening Steve DeLeo's front teeth because he asked for a match to light his Bunsen burner after Brother Vincent had told the class not to ask him for any matches.

In my third year of high school, fifth year of being paddled, and eighth year of being beaten, we students got one shot at striking back at this amazing pedagogical device. The annual drive for money for the missions was on and Father Motsko, who wanted his class to raise the most money and be rewarded with a day off, offered to let the highest bidder swat him with a paddle.

The bidding started so high ($5) most of us were eliminated on the first round, but it went up slowly after that with a milquetoast who had never been hit leading the way. We couldn't believe it. Every time one of us made a bid, he topped it. Which wouldn't have been so bad except this kid looked like he couldn't even lift Father Motsko's paddle, let alone swing it. So we began pooling our money to support the bids of Ron Allen, one of Motsko's favorite targets and capable of giving him a taste of his own medicine.

We lost. Every cent we had wasn't enough to beat this Wally Cox clone. And when it was all over, he paid for his prize with a check. Can you imagine a kid in high school having his own checking account? Were we depressed.

But then, just when things were looking up for Motsko, this Woody Allen of the west left the room and returned with the captain of the football team, an incredible bulk of muscle who made Ron Allen look like a wimp.

You could see Father Motsko was worried, but not wanting to come off as a bad sport, he bent over and "assumed the position," which is school jargon for grabbing your balls with one hand and bracing yourself against the teacher's desk with the other.

Motsko should have braced harder. Our future pro-bowler's blast lifted him up in the air and onto the top of his desk. As he lay spread-eagled on his blotter, Motsko must have wondered if he'd ever move again but, like most of those whom he had hit, he managed to hold in the pain and marvel at the burning sensation that spread across his backside.

Today I wonder if that little boy I met at St. Emeric's was awed by the same heat. I wonder if he'd like to do to me what I'd do to Brother Neri if I could get my hands on him. I wonder if by continuing the tradition of beating, I've somehow made it easier for this boy to hit his children. I wonder if he'll lose their respect the way I lost his and the students and my own. I've tried to blame what I did on my inexperience, my former teachers, and Sister Katherine, but it doesn't work. Hitting Francisco Montalvo will always be the blackest mark on my teaching record and nothing I ever accomplish will make up for it. Whether I'm lecturing on the works of Robert Coover to a tribe of Lapps or giving a reading from my novels to a group of artists at the Karolyi Foundation in France, his face is always looming out at me.

And once I hit Francisco, there was no turning back. The

kids knew my limit and seemed to go out of their way to break it. It was almost as if they derived some sort of pleasure every time I broke down and clobbered one of them.

I tried other things, like making Roberto Martinez kneel on his hands while resting his nose on the ledge of the blackboard (Sister Katherine's idea) or having the students write out "The Love Song of J. Alfred Prufrock" every time they were bad, but nothing worked. They had me and they knew it. I couldn't even take them on a field trip without their letting me get on the subway first and then waiting while the doors closed and I was taken off to our destination while they scattered in the freedom of delight.

Two students from that sixth grade class stayed in touch with me. Both are twenty-nine now, and neither has ever mentioned what a disgrace I was that first year, but they never miss an opportunity to impress my colleagues and friends by reciting "Prufrock." It's all in fun, of course, but they have no idea of the pain they cause. Like Nick Carroway, they make me realize more than anything else the futile exercise of trying to fight against the current that ceaselessly pulls us into the past.

St. Xavier High School

I didn't hit any students at St. Xavier, an all-boys Catholic high school, but I wasn't very good at stopping them from being beaten either. In my first month there, I saw young boys whipped with sticks, boards, paddles, pointers, and straps. I saw loosened teeth, swollen faces, black eyes, and what I took to be a punctured eardrum. I saw a brother walk down the corridor with his fist extended to meet anyone who wasn't keeping to his right; I saw a kid being taken to the hospital for stitches after a teacher turned him over in his desk and his head hit a radiator pipe; I saw a brother with one hand on a boy's throat and his other on the kid's balls threaten, "Now you're gonna know what it feels like to be squeezed."

Instead of stepping in and thrashing these creeps (look who's talking), I told my own students that physical punishment was against the law and if they were ever beaten they should tell their parents.

But the students didn't believe me. They thought because they were in a private school the law didn't apply. They thought their parents had given the teachers the right to hit them. The teachers were their parents away from home and had the same rights they did.

I convinced them otherwise, but they were still hesitant to do anything even though many had been slapped, paddled, or made to hold their textbooks on extended arms for various periods of time – a popular form of punishment in the school. The students said they were afraid their teachers would lower their grades or their parents wouldn't take their side.

Both excuses rang true with me. Hitting students was so common when I went to school, we didn't even question it. In time, it became a test of our masculinity. No matter how bad the pain, we refused to show any emotion. The one time I did talk about it was when my mother saw me getting out of the shower and wanted to know where the welts on my leg came from. Embarrassed at having been discovered and not wanting to get into further trouble, I played down my offence (talking when I shouldn't have been) and exaggerated the beating. Nevertheless, my mother agreed with Brother Neri: "He never would have hit you if you hadn't deserved it."

What happened to one of my students at St. Xavier was worse. He had been punched in the mouth for telling a classmate to "Fuck off," and a letter had been sent home to his father, the head of a New York mafia family. When the teacher found out whose son he had punched, he was so frightened he didn't show up at school for three days. He was even thinking of resigning and moving to his brother's on Long Island when another teacher asked the student what his father thought about the beating. The boy rolled up his shirtsleeves to show the cigarette burns on his arms. "The next time I get a letter sent home," he told the teacher, "those marks are going on my face," he said.

While burning your child for being beaten in school is an extreme reaction, the impulse is not. Many parents beat their beaten children again just to let them know whose side they're on. Of the 400 students James Michener interviewed for his book *Kent State: What Happened and Why*, 85% claimed their parents told them that, had they been protesting the R.O.T.C.'s presence on campus, it would have been a good thing if they had been shot.

Nevertheless, some parents do complain. One couple, perhaps because repairing their son's teeth required orthodontic work, went to the principal. The principal paid all the bills and a memo was then sent to the faculty reminding them it was against the law to hit a student unless in self-defense or in case of an emergency.

Almost immediately, the number of fire drills at the school went up. So did the beatings. And when the weather got too cold to go outside, the school resurrected its old air-raid drills.

But getting back at the kids periodically in the school's corridors and stairwells didn't prove very satisfactory. For one thing, the drills usually came too late after the teachers wanted to lash out, and, for another, you had to catch the kid violating some rule. Even then your punishment had to fit the crime. You couldn't, for example, just clobber a kid for all he'd been doing in your class since the last fire drill when all he'd done in this one was talk.

The best time to get in your licks now was at the student-faculty basketball game. And if you couldn't do it yourself, there was always someone on the team willing to trip a student as he drove to the basket or knock the legs out from one while he was leaping for a rebound. Before one game, I remember several teachers singling out students they wanted to hurt and planning strategies to set up a pick or box out in such a way as to make these boys vulnerable to a wild elbow or errant kick.

Whatever physical punishment took place on the basketball court, however, was nothing compared to the sexual abuse that occurred off it—something I was unaware of until I met Bryan Scholes.

Bryan was a Senior and sixth man on the varsity basketball team. Because he was trying so desperately to make the first string and win a college scholarship and, because for me basketball is cheaper than therapy, we often found ourselves playing a lot of one-on-one in the gym.

Sometimes we'd talk. Bryan had trouble sleeping at night and asked me to lend him some books. I'd give him whatever I was using in class at the time, he'd read them, and then after basketball we'd discuss them. We talked about other things too: women, drugs, the war in Viet Nam, stuff like that. One day, he told me about Brother Peter. I had read about a similar principal in James Kirkwood's *Good Times/Bad Times*, but I never believed one really existed. I didn't even believe Bryan when he told me. I kept saying he was mistaken; the principal of St. Xavier High School wouldn't risk something like that; Bryan was just suffering the effects of being in an all-boys school where everyone who didn't conform was a faggot.

I was wrong. Bryan not only answered every one of my objections, his stories were so bizarre he couldn't possibly have made them up. Like the time Brother Peter was going into the hospital for an operation on his back and wanted to take some nude pictures of Bryan to look at while he was recuperating. Peter got his pictures but Bryan made him work for them. Instead of posing on Peter's desk as the principal wanted, Bryan had him crawl about the office floor, bad back and all, and shoot up at him.

How Bryan and Brother Peter wound up in these positions began in Bryan's freshman year. Peter had his eyes on the youngster for several weeks before he got the opportunity he was looking for. He had seen Bryan enter one of the school's bathrooms and, when he didn't come out within a reasonable amount of time, the brother went in after him. Sure enough, there was smoke, and where there was smoke, there was Bryan. The boy denied that he had any cigarettes, but Brother Peter insisted that he come to his office. There, behind a locked door, the principal put into practice a technique he'd been perfecting for years: groping in boys' underwear while pretending to be searching for matches. The kids were so young (mostly freshmen but occasionally an innocent sophomore) and so afraid of getting into trouble (even if they hadn't been smoking), they didn't realize what was happening to them.

Bryan differed from these other boys in one respect: he *had* dropped his matches down his drawers as soon as he heard someone entering the lavatory. Brother Peter couldn't have been more surprised or pleased. Not only did he come off to Bryan as being pretty crafty, he found himself in the advantageous position to be merciful in victory. Instead of punishing the boy, Peter took him to lunch. Dinners at Lutecs and the Four Seasons followed. There were even a few Broadway shows thrown in. When Bryan asked how a brother could afford such luxuries, the principal told him he had a secret account into which was deposited most of the money above the school's operating expenses.

Brother Peter and Bryan quickly became good friends. Brother Peter gave Bryan late passes whenever he overslept, and he made sure Bryan was marked present for the whole day. If Bryan misbehaved in class and was sent to detention, Brother Peter let him spend the time in his office.

When Bryan's father died, Brother Peter stepped in and made all the funeral arrangements. Moreover, he found Bryan's mother a job (she had never worked before) and hired Bryan's brother (who'd recently been cut by the Nets) to coach St. Xavier's varsity basketball team. Now it was Bryan's turn to put out, to repay Brother Peter for the wonderful things he had done for him. If he didn't, his mother just might lose her job. And what was his brother going to do if he couldn't coach?

So the boy put out from the middle of his sophomore year until just before he graduated. This included summers as well. To keep tabs on him, Brother Peter hired Bryan to work in St. Xavier's summer camp for children. Bryan tried to find another job, but his mother wouldn't hear of it. What could be better than working outdoors during the summer? How could he be so ungrateful to Brother Peter?

As Bryan became more and more involved with Brother Peter, he began spending more and more time in his office. Every session repeated the last. Brother Peter would ask the boy how he was, and Bryan would tell him. Then Brother Peter would tell Bryan how beautiful he was. He'd start from Bryan's head and work downwards without ever getting to the bottom. Somewhere in between Bryan's shoulders and his thighs, Brother Peter would come from behind his desk and press Bryan up against the wall. His descriptions of Bryan's beauty turned garbled and incoherent as he forced his tongue into Bryan's mouth at every opportunity.

And what, Brother Peter wanted to know, was Bryan doing with Andersen every afternoon in the gym? We couldn't possibly be playing basketball all that time. Were we playing other games as well? Indoor games? Under the bleacher games? "Come on, Bryan, tell me, does Richard's throb for you the way mine does? How big is it? Do you want it as badly as I want yours? Give me your cock, Bryan, give it to me."

After Brother Peter got what he wanted, they'd talk. "Is there anything you need, Bryan? Are you sure you don't want some money for a malted on your way home? What are you doing Friday night?"

When I first met Bryan he was hoping Brother Peter would get him the basketball scholarship he had promised. But somehow, somewhere along the line, something had happened. Bryan had come to realize that it was he who had the power, not Brother Peter. He was the one being sought, not the principal.

Now it was Bryan's turn to dominate and control. Peter could fire anybody he wanted to, but he wouldn't see Bryan anymore. If Peter wanted nude photos to keep him company in the hospital, he'd have to crawl on the floor to take them. He'd have to suffer as much humiliation as Bryan did in posing for them.

Ironically, Bryan and Brother Peter genuinely cared for each other. Bryan saw in him a surrogate for the father he lost in his sophomore year, and it said something about Brother Peter's affection that he maintained the relationship long after he lost the upper hand. I don't think their friendship is sexual any longer—Bryan being to old to interest Peter now—but each can tell you what the other did as recently as last weekend, and they still go to restaurants and theatres together.

That Bryan wasn't Brother Peter's only love interest isn't surprising; that the principal had never been caught in his affairs is. Actually, he was caught once. One of his switchboard operators, a corps of young boys whom Peter gave the chance to earn extra money by answering the school's telephone from six to nine in the evening, couldn't make his shift one night and asked his twin brother to take his place. The brother wasn't working for an hour when Peter called him into his office. When the boy got home he told his twin, who admitted Peter had been doing the same things to him.

They decided to tell their parents. They told other people as well. Soon the whole school was waiting to see what would happen when the parents came. Teachers walked past the principal's office to see if they could hear what was going on behind the closed door, but, to everyone's surprise, nothing came of it. No one knows what he said, but Brother Peter got away with molesting *both* boys.

Never have I been in a school where people got away with more. If I saw one kid get his head banged there, I saw fifty, and the most that was ever done to stop the beatings was a weakly worded memo. If I knew of one sexual abuser, I knew of ten (all brothers, the lay teachers preferring to have affairs with and in some cases marry each other). And the one time I called the police on the Peeping Brother who had been spying every night for two weeks on the apartment I lived in across the street from the school, they didn't even take away his binoculars. The next night he was up on the roof doing the same thing.

Why didn't I do something more? I don't know. Maybe it was because Brother Peter had been the one to hire me. Maybe it was because he was the one who gave me another chance when my department chairman and the assistant principal wanted to get rid of me. Maybe it was because he was the one who gave me an after-school job to help pay for my graduate studies. Or maybe it was because I was just a coward. Whatever the reason, I'm doing something about it now, and if the right people read this, maybe things will change.

THE LOWER DECKS
Alexander Hamilton High School

Alexander Hamilton was my first public school. All the others, grammar, high, college, and the two I taught in, were Catholic. The reasons for this were my mother's wanting her son to have a Catholic education and my teachers' successful brainwashing. They taught us to feel sorry for our underprivileged brothers and sisters in the public schools, to think of them as less intelligent, morally loose, and socially inferior. Our uniforms and sense of discipline, not to mention our better penmanship, made us arrogant in the way Californians and New Yorkers frequently seem to the rest of the country or Americans appear to the rest of the world, the only difference being that our good Christian humility prevented us from being overt about it. Nevertheless, whenever we prayed before a football game or made the sign of the cross before a foul shot, we knew we always had a little of You-Know-Who's help, and that more often than not was what we believed made the difference.

Perhaps the best example of our teachers' attitudes toward public education can be expressed in the single example of my last year in grammar school. The brothers and sisters were going crazy trying to get us all into Catholic high schools. God help the poor kid they let slip into the hands of the devil. Better for any one of us to travel more than three hours every day on the subway than to walk a few blocks to the local Babylon. But try as they might, there were always a few students in each class that the good brothers and sisters couldn't get admitted. I'll never forget the look on the face of the Pastor who asked by a show of hands how many of us were going to Catholic high schools and how many weren't. When the few who hadn't made it anywhere raised their hands, a look of great sadness and pity spread across the Pastor's face and Brother Barnabas hung his head in shame. No one had to tell the elect their poor and unfortunate classmates had left the Garden of Eden.

The summer before I began teaching at St. Xavier, I was offered a job at Alexander Hamilton, but I turned it down because, in words put in my mouth at St. Xavier, I preferred not to babysit. Having been fired from Xavier for writing a petition that nobody would sign, however, babysitting didn't seem quite so unattractive, especially since my yearly salary would almost double. And whereas at St. Xavier I was expected to contribute my time to the school's extra-curricular activities, only one thing was asked of me at Alexander Hamilton: to teach from the back of the room. The principal insisted it was the soundest method for keeping the student's interest.

Aside from lecturing to the backs of a bunch of heads, Alexander Hamilton wasn't much different than I had always been told a public school would be. The students were less knowledgeable, less motivated, and less disciplined—though I envied the easy way these young men and women interacted. Perhaps predictably, the same could be said for the teachers. They punched in, punched out, and were never seen again. Nobody beat anybody else but nobody did anything they weren't paid for either. And what they did do didn't seem to amount to much.

One exception was Mrs. Rebbecca Goldburg. Mrs. Goldburg was in her last year before retirement and no two teachers contrasted as much as she and I. She was old, I was young; she was fat, I was thin; she was short, I was tall or at least taller; she was losing hair; mine came down to my shoulders.

And nowhere were we more dissimilar than in our approaches to teaching. Literally and figuratively, we were on opposite sides of the hall. Mrs. Goldburg didn't believe in relating to the students or putting on a show for them in front of the room. Nor was she very keen on whetting their interests or stirring their creativity. And preparing the "whole child" for a role in society, she left to fools.

Of these, I was probably the biggest. Willy Loman would have been proud of the way I kept my personality before my merchandise. I knew that what was important in this business was not just to be like, but to be well-liked, to sell literature through the person I wanted the students to believe I was.

Mrs. Goldburg, on the other hand, allowed literature and her students to speak for themselves by beginning each class with a ten-minute, five-question, short-answer quiz. Some of the questions were factual (to make sure they'd read the assignment), but most of them were either interpretive or associative. The interpretive questions asked the students' opinions, which had to be supported by specific references to the texts; associative questions asked the students to make connections, usually thematic, between the story they'd read for homework and previous readings.

Those poor kids! If that wasn't the most anti-all-I'd-ever-learned-about-what-it-means-to-be-a-teacher device I'd ever heard, I didn't know what was. I attracted students to *my* classes by making them exciting and fun, not by threatening the kids with quizzes and failure. My students came to class because they *wanted* to, not because they had to.

But as the semester progressed, it was Mrs. Goldburg's students who came to see their teacher (and literature) as not so bad after all. They had to come to class every day and prepare for quizzes every night, but they were also learning to enjoy reading, and they saw themselves getting better at it as they became accustomed to answering Mrs. Goldburg's questions. Instead of working against them, the quizzes were actually working for them. They gained confidence in their ability to understand and then explain what they had read. Even their writing improved.

When the final grades were posted, Mrs. Goldburg's students had the highest marks in the department. They liked being the best and showed their appreciation by dedicating the upcoming edition of the yearbook to her—the eighth time she'd received that prestigious honor.

Willyclone, meanwhile, noticed that he was liked by his students but not well enough for them to come prepared for class or even to show up if the temperature outside rose above 60 degrees. They seemed to enjoy talking about literature in the classroom, but when he met them in the halls, they were more interested in his anecdotes than anything he'd said about Hardy, Hawthorne, or Hemingway.

And what did Lomandum do about this? Nothing. He'd read the lesson plans in the *English Journal* (Mrs. Goldburg called it the *Verbal Farting*) and knew he was in step with his time. Unfortunately, there hadn't been enough of that to test the new methods accurately and he spent the whole year having discussions with the same two or three kids who always did their homework.

I don't want to go on too much longer about these quizzes, but if there's anyone reading this book who is or wants to be a teacher, they are the single, most important teaching device I've learned in the past twenty years. Their immediate advantages are obvious: the students do their homework and come to class prepared, and, within fifteen minutes, I've gotten five responses from every one of them. My biggest problem since incorporating Mrs. Goldburg's quizzes into my lesson plans has not been trying to think up ways to keep the kids' attention (the literature does that), but rather to channel their energy into a discussion that encompasses all the different approaches they take to any one work.

There is, however, one big disappointment with the quizzes. For some reason, perhaps their own immaturity, the students don't make the connection between the study habits they're made to develop in their English class and their other courses. Or rather they do, but instead of studying every subject as if they were going to be tested daily on it, they ask their teachers to discipline them by giving them more quizzes, a request that never endeared Mrs. Goldburg or me to many of our colleagues.

Sarah J. Hale High School

After I'd been "excessed" from Alexander Hamilton—a new contract had made New York's teachers the highest paid in the country but necessitated cutting back on jobs and increasing class sizes—I substituted for absent teachers in several schools, all of which had one thing in common: violence.

There were many reasons for the violence. One of them was the city's policy of integration. New York is a city of neighborhoods: Italian, Greek, Polish, German, Syrian, Jewish, Norwegian, Ukranian, Afro-American, Puerto Rican, you name it. And they each have their own schools, that is, they're city schools but most of the students in them are predominantly from one or two ethnic backgrounds. These neighborhood schools are incorporated into districts, so that in any one district, you could have a couple of Jewish schools, a Scandnavian school, and say, an Italian school. Now one of the things a district with this kind of configuration wants to do is preserve the ethnic integrity of its schools. To do this at a time when white middle-class families are moving to the suburbs and the black and Puerto Rican population is bursting at the seams of their ghettos is no easy task. The principals can't say they don't have the room. And they can't say the inner city's schools aren't overcrowded and understaffed. So what these mostly white districts have done is sacrificed one of their schools to the blacks and Puerto Ricans, absorbed the displaced whites in the remaining schools, and enrolled enough minorities—mostly athletes and the students with the highest learning potential—to make everything look respectable. On paper, the total student population of these districts is admirably integrated, but in reality . . . ?

In reality, you can't fool the students—not the ones in the predominantly black and Puerto Rican schools anyway. They see declining property values tabulating in the eyes of the whites as they pass between the subway and their school, they feel the rush given them by store owners trying to hang onto their local customers, and they see it in the tired, bored, condescending looks of the older teachers who remember the way it was. It's also in the eyes and frequently in the hands and more than a few times in the penises of the "un-excessed" younger teachers who aren't as cautious as they would be with white students from their own neighborhoods. In one school, I met two teachers, both in their late twenties, who claimed they'd been sleeping with between thirteen and eighteen students a year for the past five years. Encouraging me to take advantage of this sex mine, they stressed the sensuousness of the blacks, the *salsa* of the Puerto Ricans, and the almost uncanny loyalty of both to their teachers.

To their other teachers and themselves, the students weren't so considerate. I was helping a teacher hang some artwork in one school's lobby when out of the corner of my eye, I saw two girls taking off their "fuck-me shoes" and placing them next to the wall. I didn't think anything of it—except how impractical platform shoes were for hanging artwork—and continued with my work.

All of a sudden, students started screaming and running past me. There was a fight at the other end of the hall. I rushed to break it up, but the students had locked arms in a circle around two fighting girls, and I couldn't get through. I finally had to crawl over more than a half dozen shoulders to get to the center. Blood, ripped clothes, and snatches of hair were everywhere.

I managed my way between the shoeless fighters, but somehow they were able to reach around me and grab each other's hair. And pull. By the time some other teachers came and separated them, each girl had a lock of hair in her hands that was several inches thick.

We marched them to the principal's office, but neither girl would say what the fight was about. I later discovered from one of my own students that it was over a teacher who'd been sleeping with both of them. Whether the principal knew this or not, he did nothing. It was in his interest to suppress information about violence rather than risk any adverse publicity. Several months later, when one of these girls tried to stab a different girl who was having an affair with the same teacher, the principal suspended her. No other action was taken.

In some schools, the students took the law into their own hands. At Sarah J. Hale, named in honor of the woman responsible for making Thanksgiving a national holiday, there was a pretty girl who was continuously harassed by a group of young boys. No matter where she went, they seemed to be there: pulling her hair, knocking her books out of her arms, stealing her dessert, anything they could think of to make her notice them.

She was standing in line in the cafeteria one day when one of the boys got in line behind her. Showing off for his friends at a nearby table, he began putting everything on her tray back where it came from. Each time she retrieved one thing, something else was missing.

His friends cracked up, laughing and cheering and applauding even louder when he began putting things *on* the girl's tray. Five milks instead of one, six cupcakes instead of two, that sort of thing. By the time the girl got to the cash register, her tray was a cornucopia of cafeteria food.

The cashier began ringing it all up.

That's when it happened.

Reaching inside her jacket, the girl pulled out a straight-edged razor and began slicing up the boy's face.

He was so stunned he just stood there while she cut away at him.

The cashier didn't even notice. She just kept ringing up the sales.

Finally someone screamed and all hell broke loose. The boys ran to rescue their friend, who had recovered by now and was trying to defend himself, while the students rushed to form themselves into a circle.

The teacher on duty rushed to stop the fight, but a student blindsided him with a chair.

Someone pulled the fire alarm.

The kitchen workers ran for the door.

Teachers on the outside bolted it to contain the riot.

That afternoon, I was hired to replace not the gym teacher who had his kneecap shattered in the cafeteria, but Miss Finkle, a freshman science teacher, who got two of her ribs broken in a separate incident.

What I knew about science couldn't fill the bottom of a teacup, but it didn't matter. The Board of Education was giving combat pay to anyone who'd stay in the same room with these kids. The trouble was the kids wouldn't stay in the room. They'd break holes into the walls that only they were small enough to crawl through and, once inside, it was party time: getting high, rapping with friends, and mimicking the pleas of their teachers to come out and learn.

The Dean of Students told me to ignore them: "They're just looking for attention. Once they see you're not going to give them any—no matter how repulsive they may become—they'll be out."

But these kids didn't need my attention. As soon as I stopped trying to communicate with them, they turned on their ghetto blasters. I couldn't think, let alone hear myself speak, and the smell of marijuana wafting into the room was as thick as perfume in a Paris Metro.

Finally, security arrived. They enlarged a few holes and went after the kids, most of whom escaped through the endless maze connecting every room on the floor. The three that were captured (all from my class) were taken to the dean and immediately returned. There was such a long line of kids waiting to be disciplined, they had been told to wait in their classroom until they were called.

They entered the room with their music blaring, which turned on the other students as well. What did they care if an egg was a single cell? It was their bodies that wanted to move, not their brains.

And could those bodies move! Disco, break, even the jitterbug. It made me want to dance too. But I couldn't (at least not all the time), and they knew they couldn't get away with it forever, so we made a deal. If they'd let me teach them science for thirty-five minutes every day, I'd let them teach me how to dance for fifteen.

We got along pretty well after that, though I'm sure I learned more than they did. Later, I made another deal with them. If they passed a test every Thursday, I'd take them on a field trip every Friday. But the whole class had to pass. If one student failed, the trip was off.

Three exams later, we were on the BMT to Manhattan. Music and kids bounced off the seats and walls like so many atoms bombarding one another. Not having been to the Museum of Natural History and Hayden Planetarium since I was a Cub Scout, I was bouncing too.

Only when we got out of the subway, the kids changed. They were on new turf and it frightened them. Even the radios were silent. They began holding on to me, each one touching me somehow, somewhere, to make sure I didn't run away and leave them.

I promised I wouldn't abandon them, but that wasn't good enough. Finally, we agreed that two people could link arms with me and we would form a chain as we walked. This didn't leave much room for anybody else on the sidewalk, but at least we were walking instead of stumbling over one another.

Two women passed us from the opposite direction. They smiled at the teacher out for a day with his students. The teacher smiled back.

The next thing I knew four or five girls in the class had pressed these women up against a gate. "Who do you think you are, lookin' at our teacher, lady?" "What you think you smilin' at?" "You want your face slapped or what?"

I apologized to the women and had to threaten to run away if the girls didn't follow. What they'd done was embarrassing, but in a way it felt good. These were the toughest kids I'd ever known (four of them would die violently within the next two years), and here they were being afraid and affectionate in ways I could never have imagined.

Back at school, however, it was always the same. They worked a little and cheated a lot (the closest some of them ever got to science), but trouble was never more than a few seconds away, and anything could set it off: A fight, a student wandering into the room looking for a friend, a pen that belonged to someone else, anything.

One day, I asked the students why they fought so much. Didn't they realize they were only showing how much they hated themselves? I didn't know whether this was true, but it sounded good, and I thought it might help if they believed they were really hitting themselves whenever they lashed out at someone else.

For the first time, there was silence in the room. For the first time, they were thinking about something other than how many more minutes before they got to dance. For the first time, I had gotten through to them. It was like magic.

When the bell rang, we walked down the stairs and out of the building together. I don't think I had ever felt so good about anything I'd ever done.

Then it happened. Another fight. Only this time it broke out right in front of us, and, when the circle formed, I was in the middle. Sharing the ring were two students and a mother. Built like a planet, the mother was encouraging her daughter to kick the shit out of a girl about a third her size. Or maybe it was to crush her because that was what the daughter was doing. Only the smaller girl's feet and hands were visible.

But she was a fighter. When I bent over to try to lift the fat girl off her, the little one began pulling on my pantleg with her teeth, jerking her head like a dog in a tug of war.

Then it was the mother's turn to attack. Who did I think I was butting my nose into what was none of my business?

I looked for some other teachers to help me, but they were scrambling from the parking lot like so many lemmings.

The mother began screaming that no one was going to say her daughter was pregnant and get away with it.

Spreading my feet as far away from the skinny girl's teeth as possible, I tried to roll the fat girl off her.

That's when the mother began hitting me with her umbrella.

And that's when the students in my class attacked the mother.

And that's when some of the other kids, thinking the sides were unfair, jumped in.

And that's when I heard the sirens, and the police came, and I got hit on the head, and was arrested for being an outside agitator.

III

Manning the Pumps

In 1983, the National Commission on Excellence in Education announced that the country was in big trouble. A "rising tide of mediocrity" (to put it mildly) was taking over our schools, and something had to be done about it. Since then, more than thirty national reports on education, over two hundred and ninety state commissions, several television documentaries, some pretty extensive media coverage, and a major motion picture have all offered their particular programs of reform.

Not one of them will make more than a dent in solving the problem of why Mr. Johnny can no longer teach. The reasons are two: The distance separating the experts from the schools and the resistance of teachers to change.

I don't know how many people have sat on how many commissions since 1983, but I can bet very few of them have ever spent much time teaching in a public school. And why should they? Research is where the credit and money are. The University of Chicago recognized this in 1975 when it closed its teacher-training program for being unscholarly. And who could blame them? In a field where the schools of education are rated by the number of times their professors' names appear in scholarly footnotes, producing good teachers doesn't amount to very much. At Stanford and the University of California at Berkeley, for example, seventy percent of the faculty have never taught in a public school, and an even greater percentage of their students have no intention of teaching whatsoever. Is it any wonder, then, that a committee of twenty-five scholars and educators, calling themselves "The Thanksgiving Group" because of the time at which they released their manifesto in 1984, could call for parental choice in the selection of schools, the abolishment of undergraduate teacher-training programs, and more emphasis on character development in the schools? Since when did parents, unless they were financially or geographically handicapped, not have a strong voice in selecting which schools their children should attend? And what good does abolishing teacher-training programs do? Isn't some training better than none? Or couldn't the existing programs be improved? Do they have to be abolished? Doesn't that sound like a rather ineffective way to deal with the problem? Eliminate it by abolishing it? And what about our students' character development? How can teachers develop their students' characters when they can't even teach them to read or write? Shouldn't first things come first?

Yes and no. Even though the proposals of the Thanksgiving Group may seem like the reflections of so many ivy-towered theorists, they are right on target. Or at least pretty close to it. But like their students who learn the general rules of child psychology and not how and when to apply a certain technique to a certain group of children to achieve a certain response, the Thanksgiving Group failed to translate its theories into individual circumstances. Like so many officers on a bridge, they have a good view of the ship's direction but can't see what's going on down below.

And yet, it is down below where any sustained improvement must originate. Teachers and parents must *recognize* their problems and *want* to do something about them. Without that recognition and desire, all the bureaucratic mandates from above will only cause more confusion.

Given the condition of our schools presented in the previous pages of this book, strength of will may seem like an overly simplistic response to incompetency, indifference, ignorance, inflexibility, insecurity, and child abuse. Perhaps it is, but in my twenty years of teaching, I've never been in a school that couldn't significantly improve its performance by simply deciding to do so.

One small example. Ask any teacher in this country which instructional period is his least favorite (as opposed to the class he hates the most), and almost invariably his answer will be the last. The reasons are obvious: He's already struggled through four classes as well as the bureaucratic hassles that fill up his two free periods: attendance (a major undertaking in many schools), announcements, extra curricular activities, and paperwork thrust at him from health officials (everything from vaccinations to cavities), social workers, insurance companies (how did that window on the third floor really break?), truant officers, the guidance department, athletic coaches (will Johnny be eligible to play?), and divorce lawyers (which parent is better for Mary?). Even the task as fundamental as evaluation can become overwhelming. In Atlanta, for example, fourth- and fifth-grade teachers are expected to rate their students on sixty separate skills ranging from whether they can write ideas clearly to whether they can apply "scarcity, opportunity cost and resource allocation to local, national, and global situations." With jargon like that to wade through, is it any wonder that most teachers want to get through their final periods of the day with as little trouble as possible?

Getting through the last period with as little trouble as possible, however, often means striking a deal with the students, who are also tired but also excited that the day is almost over and soon they'll be free to play ball or hang out with their friends. They want to make the last period go quickly too. And what's the best way of doing that? By distracting their teachers into a conversation about their families, their pasts, the upcoming game, the day's newspaper headlines—anything that will keep them from doing what they're supposed to be doing.

Now the teachers know what the students are up to. They're no fools; they were students once themselves. But they also know how much easier it is to give in, to avoid trouble, to let themselves be heard expounding about all the subjects on which they are authorities. Ironically, it is the things said during these weaker moments that the students remember most. Years later, they won't recall a single point you made concerning *Julius Caesar*, the Battle of the Bulge, or the rights of minorities, but they'll repeat word for word the time you got on the plane to Hawaii without your husband.

Few teachers are very proud of these moments, but most

schools refuse to do anything to help them. One exception, St. Xavier High School, decided to rotate its schedule of periods so that the first period on Monday became the second on Tuesday and so on for eight periods. Not only did each faculty member have to teach only one final period every eight days, but every teacher got to come in late and go home early four times every week and a half. Of course the students still had to come in and leave on time, but with their last period of the day always being a different class, they couldn't count on distracting the same teacher day after day. In fact, the teachers began saving their examinations and in-class essays for the final periods. As good a technique as any for keeping the students in their seats and concentrating on their work, the examinations helped the students become better students and, because they were now correcting more papers than before, the teachers became better teachers.

So there you have it—a simple solution to a perennial problem made possible because the teachers were willing to do something about it. Granted they were more interested in making life easier on themselves than helping the students, but if the quality of instruction and learning improves, does the reason always matter? More important, will this work in your school?

Probably not. And probably for the same reason it was rejected in the five high schools I taught in after I left St. Xavier, namely, because those teachers who have paid their dues and earned schedules that enable them to come in late or leave early don't want to share what they consider to be their just reward. And as for any teacher who doesn't give the same kind of class in his last period as he does in his first, these old teachers with short memories often reply, well that's just plain unprofessional. He should be fired.

As important as will is to change, however, nothing ensures success quite so easily as an active Parent-Teacher Association. I can't emphasize enough the enormous degree of pressure that parents can bring to improving teaching. Unfortunately, I can't cite a single personal example of this influence because—with the exception of sports programs—most parents just don't care. Their share of the responsibility seems to end when they get their kids out of the house in the morning, which wouldn't be so bad if the kids could be responsible for their own educations, but they can't and neither can the teachers. With more than thirty-five percent of our mothers working full-time, teachers have seen support for their efforts weakened by reduced parental supervision and their own responsibilities increased by the many family problems that have been subsequently dumped in their laps. Today's teachers are expected to be mother, father, priest, shrink, police officer, playground monitor, and cafeteria supervisor. They're expected to compensate for racial prejudice, economic inequality, and societal indifference, and now, when they're not teaching Johnny to read or Mary to write, the Thanksgiving Group wants them to develop their students' characters as well. Is it any wonder, then, that in the past fifteen years, the number of teachers with twenty years or more experience has dropped by half, that four out of ten claim they will quit before retirement, and that over two-thirds would rather be doing something else?

I remember one school in which the students brought a bum in off the street and sat him in the back of the room. Mistaking him for a parent, the teacher gave her best class in years and her first in weeks that wasn't pure "busy work" assigned straight from the textbook. The students learned a lesson too—one bum in the classroom was enough.

But think what the effect would be if every parent took one day off a year to go to school with his child? Parents would show that they care, teachers would no longer feel they were alone in a losing battle against an indulgent age, and students might actually learn something. As long as society continues to care more about championships and diplomas than education, however, society is going to continue to get the schools it deserves.

In spite of this condition, there are *some* schools where the principals are more interested in leading their teachers than in protecting themselves, where the teachers are more committed to teaching basic skills than waxing eloquent on the theories they learned in college, and where parents are asked to contribute more than money. In these schools, and it doesn't matter whether the kids are rich, poor, black, white, or green, expectations become high, standards are raised, order pervades, and *everybody* (students, parents, *and* teachers) learns.

Without communal support and the desire to improve, however, there will be no salvation for most of our nation's schools. There are just too many with too many problems for any governor, legislature, university, or school superintendent to be of any significant influence. With society's support, on the other hand, there are a few things that we all—parents, teachers, administrators, taxpayers, and government officials—can do to encourage reform and development.

1. Eliminate the Bad

When I was teaching at Boston University's College of Basic Studies, there was a professor who had been given tenure even though he hadn't completed his doctorate, had never published so much as a "Letter to the Editor," and consistently received low marks on his students' evaluations. During faculty meetings, he used to sit near the coffee machine and carve designs in the styrofoam cups with a penknife. At a meeting between the Humanities and Science Departments to try to find some inter-disciplinary topics that could generate greater student interest in both subjects, he refused to participate. Some said it was because he didn't want to change his syllabus; others said he didn't like the Science Department; most didn't know. Whatever the reason, he just turned his back on the whole proceeding and carved away. Perhaps he was thinking about his duties as a member of the Merit Committee, whose charge it was to evaluate which professors had earned, through teaching, publication, and service to the college, an increase in their salaries.

At a better-than-average institution like the College of Basic Studies, there are only a handful of these professors, but in many schools they are the norm. I know teachers who daily give their students a multiple-choice exam on the previous night's homework, allow them to correct each others' papers, and then read aloud the grades they've received for recording. The exams are never collected and no check is made to see if the reported grades coincide with the given ones. Perhaps these teachers are trying to develop their students' characters. Perhaps they're succeeding. I don't know, but most of them are convinced they've developed a perfect instructional system: homework every night to please the parents, quizzes every day to keep the students in their seats, and plenty of grades to show their administrators if need be. And all these teachers have to do is mimeograph, read the newspaper, record the grades, and collect their paychecks.

Not all bad teachers are lazy or lack interest, however. Some try very hard and are extremely interested in their students' performances. In one of the schools I worked in, the final examinations in the federally supported remedial program had to be corrected by "outside" readers, so I and a few other substitute teachers got to earn some extra money for Christmas. We were given a dollar for every exam we finished and were told we could knock off twenty in an hour if we didn't read them very carefully. We were also told that the jobs of the people who taught these remedial courses depended on how many students failed. So every time we gave an "F," we had to tell a monitor in the front of the room who kept a count of the failures on her blackboard, and every time she had enough failures to make up a class, the remedial teachers, who were on hand to "help" us, cheered.

Now I don't know how much the other graders were affected by this, but when I heard so many "F's" being called out, I thought I was being too lenient. And of the six exams I was unsure about, the remedial teachers encouraged me to give them "F's." "Better that they should really know how to read and write," one explained, "than be passed on to work they may not be prepared to handle."

I did what I was told because I thought the teachers knew best, and I was grateful to them for giving me the opportunity to earn extra money. I didn't want to ruin their Christmas by taking away their jobs, but later, when they took us to dinner, I couldn't get the image out of my mind of their getting up every morning, coming to school, and working real hard at *not* teaching the students how to read and write.

There are a lot of bad teachers out there, and they're not going to go away on their own. Competency testing won't get rid of them either; they've already blocked that through their unions and professional associations. What's needed in many cases is a strong principal, someone who is willing to risk his popularity in long and costly grievances. Unfortunately, many principals come from the same mold as the bad teachers and aren't willing to erode their own support by making waves. It's easier to get rid of the good teachers, the ones who threaten everyone else's mediocrdity.

In an earlier chapter, I told the story of a gifted science teacher whose assistant principal and department chairman did not have the capacity to understand or appreciate him. What I didn't mention was the teacher who was given tenure instead: a graduate of Columbia University who rarely came to school on time, never prepared for classes, often showed up stoned or hung over, couldn't control his students, and spent many of his free periods getting high or watching television. Why was he chosen over the other? Two reasons: He was like most of the other teachers on the faculty, and the principal wasn't willing to overrule the recommendations of his assistant and department chairman even though he admired the science teacher's work. Having chosen his assistant and chairman for their limited minds and his ability to manipulate them, he was now stuck with their decision. As good a teacher as the principal knew Jim Anton to be, it was wiser to maintain his good relationship with the others.

2. Improve the Rest

This is easier said than done. At the end of my first year at Boston University, my students' evaluations were among the highest in the college, and I was invited to join the Committee to Improve Teaching. The committee had been meeting regularly, attending faculty improvement conferences all over the country, reading the latest developments in the field, and failing to pass a single measure through the faculty-at-large for three years. Part of the problem was the committee itself. It included a professor whose student evaluations vied with the coffee-cup sculptor's for the lowest ranking in the college as well as a professor who believed teaching was a natural gift rather than a learned skill. "You either have it or you don't," he continually repeated. Then there was the chairman, a well-intentioned man who frequently wondered aloud at meetings why his fly wouldn't stay up, and I, a newcomer whose program of daily quizzes had already caused some teachers to complain that their students were so busy studying for humanities, they couldn't devote sufficient time to anything else.

By the end of that year, the committee came up with another proposal they hoped the faculty would accept: Hire an independent team of authorities from Kansas State University, which offered such a program, to come to the College of Basic Studies, videotape each teacher in his classroom, and then in a private viewing conference, show each teacher where he could improve his instructional techniques. No one would know anything about how any other teacher performed, the tapes would either be erased or given to the teachers after the conference, and it would be up to each teacher to accept or reject the advice he had been given.

The proposal was overwhelmingly defeated. For one thing, it cost money that might be better spent on something else — like a decent photocopy machine. For another, how did we know these people were capable of evaluating such a specialized faculty as the one at the College of Basic Studies? And if they were really that good, what were they doing at Kansas State?

In spite of such resistance, however, principals and department heads can bring pressure to bear on teachers whose classes amount to little more than busy work. Everyone knows who they are; the problem is that there are so many of them. And that problem will continue to get worse as long as principals fire teachers who threaten the status quo, students prefer easy to challenging courses, and parents don't care what their children learn as long as they pass.

Textbook publishers, eager to give everyone what they so obviously want, are falling over themselves in the rush to produce books that promise less work for everybody—especially the teachers who order them. Writing in the introduction to an anthology of essays they edited for composition classes, Harry Brent and William Lutz tell us: "We saw them (teachers of writing): walking across the campus with evil expressions as they carried great piles of themes, rubber bands popping everywhere, grim with the knowledge that their weekends would be spent matching errors against a grammar chart. We did not look forward to the prospect of meeting our writing teachers on Monday morning."

You don't want to be one of these teachers, do you? Buy our book and learn how to keep your weekends free *and* be popular with your students at the same time.

"We all know that to improve our writing we need not only to read but to write, and to write regularly. We also know that large classes and heavy teaching schedules" (mostly teachers believe they have either or both) "make it very difficult to assign or to write well large numbers of formal essays in the course of a semester.

"We have kept this contradiction in mind while writing this book. The questions after each selection have been formulated not only to clarify the structure of the essay they follow but also to stimulate brief in-class writing assignments that need not be formally graded by the instructor." (Read: Here's how to fill up class time with busy work.) "We suggest that after reading and discussing a selection from *The Perennial Reader* students answer selected discussion questions in writing . . . Our experience suggests that these assignments: (1) be done in a limited time period; (2) be shared with other students in the same class for comments and revision; and (3) not be graded as formal writing assignments . . .

"In addition to our desire to make comfortable writing activities a part of every writing class, three other premises underlie our approach . . . : (1) not all writing assignments ought to be formally graded; (2) students can honestly collaborate with their peers in selected in-class prewriting and writing activities; and (3) the final draft of an essay may be preceded by several revisions of earlier drafts, which, where collaborative learning takes place, the instructor does not have to comment on in detail."

The four paragraphs I've excerpted here appear on two consecutive pages in *The Perennial Reader*, and even though Brent and Lutz promise "other premises," their message is the same: our book means less work for the teacher.

That the students should do most of the work in their own writing classes is as it should be, but who do Brent and Lutz think they're fooling? Even a novice teacher knows that "students can honestly collaborate with their peers" but more often than not either aren't likely to or don't know how to. And though they may incorporate another student's grammatical corrections (right or wrong) into their papers, most students are not going to re-write anything. When they finish typing an essay from its rough draft, they're usually so happy to be rid of the pain of having prepared it for submission, they're only interested in the grade they're going to receive. On the other hand, many students *are* willing to rewrite a paper to improve a grade, but you won't find this sequence in Brent and Lutz's program. Their technique is to come up with ways to delay the final submissions and to relieve teachers of the detailed comments that many students need to rewrite their papers. In Brent and Lutz's program, the teachers don't read anything twice.

Who, then, are they fooling? Perhaps it's the publisher who looks constantly for a selling point and thinks he can capitalize on teacher laziness, but I doubt it. My guess is that Brent and Lutz aren't fooling anybody, and that a lot of their sales are going to come from teachers who are looking for ways to get out of investing the time and energy necessary to improve students' writing.

One of Brent and Lutz's recommendations, ironically, is frequent quizzes on the readings that can be corrected while the students are completing an assignment in class. Rather than challenge the students with questions that will make them express real thoughts, however, as Mrs. Goldburg did, Brent and Lutz require only one-word answers that serve no greater purpose than making sure the students have done their homework. The suggested quiz for "The Declaration of Independence," for example, includes questions like "What are the inalienable rights all men are endowed with?" instead of "Do we in America have inalienable rights? Support your answer with specific examples from your own life or books you have read." Instead of asking the students to define what they mean by a tyrant within a given context, Brent and Lutz ask, "What harsh term is applied to the King of England?"

The most recent book I've read in this field has substituted student essays for those by professional writers. Learning to write from these lesser models, the editors imply, is as easy as walking down a flight of stairs, and Marcel Duchamp's gracefully flowing "Nude Descending a Staircase" underscores this point on the book's cover.

Unfortunately, learning to write is not as easy as descending a staircase. In addition to the many "natural" writing techniques developed over the last ten years, writing requires a commitment to basic skills that most teachers and students just don't want to make. Why students may not wish to participate in anything more vigorous than watching television is understandable, but why teachers who are supposed to know the importance of basic skills continue to avoid them is less so. Perhaps, like those in the publishing industry, they've learned there's more to be gained by giving people what they want. Look at it from their point of view. If an instructor goes into a classroom prepared to teach a fundamental skill in writing, he knows three things before he opens the door: (1) his students aren't going to like it; (2) they're probably going to become bored very quickly; and (3) if they become bored, they're going to make trouble for him. Isn't it easier on everybody concerned for the teacher to talk about a story he's assigned instead? Even if they haven't read it, he can keep them entertained by paraphrasing the highlights in terms they can appreciate and later feel like he's accomplished something when he reads his own words fed back to him on an exam. The time goes by quickly, the students don't act up, and the teacher comes off as smart and cool instead of authoritative and dull. Everybody's happy, and nobody remembers anything two months after the last day of class.

3. Reward the Good

Rewarding the good teachers may be the easiest, most effective, and least expensive way to encourage all teachers to improve their performances. Unfortunately, public recognition of good teachers is not a popular sentiment.

Years ago, feminists introduced the word "shitwork," which means work that's noticed only if it's done poorly. A husband can come home weeks on end and not say anything about his house, his dinner, or his kids, but the one time the living room is a mess, his potatoes are cold, or his child is misbehaving at the table, his wife hears about it.

Teaching is the same way. You only hear about the work you're doing badly. When I first started teaching, the only comments I received on my chairman's observations were things like "a student in the third row was chewing gum" and "too many of the windows were closed." On my last observation, it was reported that I let three women come in late for class, the implication being that I'm lax on attendance. But what the observer didn't know was that these women all had children at home and couldn't leave the house until their babysitters arrived. One of them had to work a night shift, rush home to help her husband get the older children off to school, and then wait for the babysitter. That these women managed to show up every day for their eight o'clock class amazed me to no end, but when the chairman reads his observer's report, will he wonder why these women were late, or like the husbands feminists complain about, will he only see what he perceives to be deficiencies in my authority? The answer is neither. He'll ask me to explain why the women came late, and I'll tell him, but all he'll remember is that they came in late because that's what he's being paid to notice—the shitwork.

In a job that most people didn't enter for the money, praise means a great deal—a yearbook dedication, an alumni award, a teacher-of-the-year trophy, a note of congratulations on the results of your students' evaluation, anything that can make you feel like you're appreciated by somebody. Raj Chopra, the superintendent of schools in Council Bluffs, Iowa, has gone even further to meet this teachers' need. He helped raise his district's S.A.T. scores after they had fallen below the national standard by starting a campaign to encourage "positive thinking" by and about teachers. One of the things he came up with was a Teachers Recognition Day on which retailers give discounts to teachers. Says Chopra: "We try to make teachers feel proud of their profession by emphasizing that what they do will have an impact on the country for years to come."

A more professional way to reward good teachers and improve others at the same time is through incentive plans based on performance and ability rather than longevity and educational level. In Tennessee, for example, a teacher can earn a $1,000 bonus, a $2,000, or a $3,000 bonus for a ten-month contract, $5,000 for eleven months, and $7,000 for a twelve-month contract. Of the state's 41,000 teachers, 39,000 have applied for the program.

In addition to rewarding its best teachers with bonuses, California has dubbed some of them "mentors," a title that carries with it an additional $2,000 to carry out any number of new responsibilities ranging from helping other teachers to developing the curriculum. The first full year the program was in operation, 3,568 of the state's 178,133 teachers served as mentors.

One advantage of these programs, in addition to improving the quality of education on every level, is that it keeps good teachers in the classroom, the traditional route having been to move into the more powerful and remunerative administrative positions. The program's biggest problem, on the other hand, is developing a system that can evaluate and choose the superior teachers fairly. In a field top-heavy with mediocrity, it may be a long time before those other than the mediocre will be rewarded.

A cheaper way to recognize good teachers that would also give them a sense of respect, accomplishment, and power would be to pay their expenses for conferences, summer fellowships, and individual study projects. Although this form of recognition and improvement is not probable in a time of cutbacks and retrenchment, school boards can create in-service programs that will bring about some of the same results at very little expense. Run by the best teachers to help others improve instructional skills, in-service workshops such as the model program in Lincoln, Nebraska, give teachers with common interests and problems an opportunity to meet the needs their more broadly-ranged schools of education failed to provide. Instead of having to glean what they can from such diverse, undefined, and useless courses as "Puppetry," "Descriptive Linguistics," and "Life Style of the High School Student," teachers can discuss ways to make algebra interesting or teach acceptable social routines to handicapped students.

Unlike most in-service programs, which are taught by local college professors or outside experts, the courses administered in Lincoln are run by Lincoln teachers who have achieved success in dealing with the problems of Lincoln students. In addition, there is an eleven-member "helping-teacher cadre" of practicing teachers who are available at any time to work with fellow teachers on any problem too specialized or personal for a regular workshop. Only when the teachers themselves are at a loss to solve their own problems is an outside expert called in. Even then, however, the choices of what techniques are employed are left to the teachers.

And what about the good teachers? Aside from professional conferences and summer fellowships, are there any ways to improve their skills? In addition to what they can learn from their colleagues as "mentors" and "leaders," our country's best teachers can benefit from faculty exchanges across the country and throughout the world. By exchanging houses and cars as well as jobs, the costs of transportation and salary differentials could be picked up by the schools. In most cases, this would amount to less than the bonuses they are currently awarding good teachers.

Aside from a few programs administered mostly for college professors, however, faculty exchanges are mostly unheard of, and yet they are a vital stimulus to good teaching. This is especially true for people who have spent more than ten years at a single institution. Even the best of teachers tend to settle in and grow stale after this much time. With the same colleagues, teaching the same kinds of courses to the same kinds of students, it's almost inevitable. A year at another school, however, gives a teacher an opportunity to assume a new position without losing his old job. Returning with the fresh set of viewpoints that an exchange affords, teachers more often than not are eager to apply the new techniques they've learned from feedback with students and teachers to their old turfs. Not only do these teachers benefit, but so do their students and schools. Unfortunately, there is no organization in the United States that administers intranational exchanges, and most teachers aren't interested in finding individual replacements on their own.

4. Recruit the Promising

Not an easy task in a profession that most people consider a dead end with no money, but a challenge that must be met if we hope to improve our schools and the quality of education they offer.

In spite of a current shortage of teachers in math and science and predicted shortages in other fields, the number of people entering the teaching profession has declined steadily since 1979. It's little wonder. The average starting salary of $14,026 is well below what college graduates entering business and industry are paid, and the average pay of all teachers at $22,000 offers little incentive for a long-term commitment. Add to this the almost universally poor working conditions and lack of respect for the profession and you have schools like Duke University closing their education departments because there aren't enough students to keep it open.

Admission to the remaining schools of education is almost a foregone conclusion. With the combined S.A.T. score of high school seniors intending to teach now at 812 out of a possible 1600 (well below the national average and falling), most schools no longer consider the S.A.T., which wouldn't be so bad if nine schools in ten hadn't also dropped the high school class rank and grade point average as criteria for acceptance in teacher education.

And getting out is easier than getting in. Only forty-seven percent of the education schools in this country require an exit exam, and only five percent of those test academic subjects. What, then, do would-be teachers learn in their four years of college? Not much, according to James D. Koerner, vice president of the Alfred P. Sloan Foundation. In his book, *The Miseducation of American Teachers,* Koerner tells us the field "has not developed a corpus of knowledge and technique of sufficient scope and power to warrant the field's being given full academic status." Basically the same in the nature of their content for the past fifty years, education courses make up about thirty to forty percent of the undergraduate credits of an elementary education major and about twenty to thirty percent of the credits of a secondary education major. Nevertheless, according to a recent Harris Poll, only ten percent of all teachers agree that their training did a good job of preparing them for the classroom, and even Albert Shanker, president of the American Federation of Teachers, admits that education "is the only professional field where after people graduate they say they could have been better off without the training."

The Thanksgiving Group of 1984 and Carnegie Commission of 1986 recognizes that most education schools are little more than diploma mills set up to satisfy state certification requirements and make money for the colleges, but abolishing them as they suggest won't solve the problem. As dim as most teachers' understanding of history and algebra may be, there is something to be said for well developed blackboard skills.

A more effective solution, however might be to change the schools themselves, to raise their standards of recruitment, curriculum, and graduation, and to threaten the accreditation of schools that fall below par. There are many ways to go about doing this and some important work has already been started, most notably at Harvard and Illinois State Universities. Few programs, however match the one established at the University of New Hampshire.

To begin with, no one gets to sign up for a course in education until they've completed a baccalaureate degree in some academic subject, thus insuring a basic grasp of whatever the teacher intends to instruct. To emphasize the importance of knowing what you're talking about would sound ludicrous if it weren't for the fact that most education school graduates are so blatantly ignorant of almost anything beyond the unintelligible jargon of their own pedagogy.

Teachers, as a group, aren't believed to be the dumbest of all professionals for nothing; they've earned the marks that have placed them well below the arts and sciences. And the jargon they've created to make themselves sound professional—terms like "congenital prestige deprivation" for "lack of respect," for example—have only added to the damage. The most damaged of all, however, are the students whose potential for clear thinking and expression is being partially sabotaged by people who can't think or communicate clearly themselves.

Elementary school teachers argue that it isn't necessary for them to know any single subject well because of the achievement levels of their students and the fact that they are asked to teach a broad range of subjects. Many educators, perhaps fearing their teachers might find their work boring or frustrating if they developed too much interest in any one subject, agree.

Let's say for the sake of argument that they're right. Perhaps a special undergraduate degree, modelled on the regular undergraduate degree programs in some Scandinavian countries, for example, could be created for those intending to become elementary school teachers. In such a program, the students would choose three subjects and then, after a year of general courses not in these fields, study each chosen subject for a year with a degree of science or arts being awarded in the field with the most courses. A student, then, could choose, say, English, math and history, or science, math and English, or psychology, math, and science or any combination of any subjects he wished to teach. He would then, after that first year of study intended to broaden his perspectives and provide a basis for the work to follow, take all the courses of his sophomore year in one subject, followed by all the courses in his junior year in a second, and so on. Or perhaps these subjects could be divided into thirty credits each to be taken in any order at any time. The sequence doesn't matter all that much. What is important, though, is what no prospective teachers be allowed to apply to schools of education until they've earned their Bachelor Degrees. And even then it probably wouldn't be a bad idea to require them to sit for a national test similar to the ones would-be doctors and lawyers have to take.

Before they can enter the University of New Hampshire's School of Education, every student must earn a liberal arts degree and work as a teacher's aide during his sophomore year, an early exposure to the classroom that eliminates about fifty percent of the students and strengthens the commitment of the other fifty. During the summer following their senior year, the students take two graduate education courses as well as participate in weekly seminars offering advice on everything from how to handle disruptive children to how to live on a salary of $13,000 a year. A full-year's unpaid teaching internship follows with another summer of courses and seminars to be completed before certification is granted. The result is a group of people who have something to say *and* know how to say it.

Unfortunately, most students aren't willing to commit themselves to five years of work when they can be certified everywhere else in four. And most schools of education aren't willing to sacrifice tuition for standards, which is why the changes in the ways we train our teachers must be across the board. Until that day comes, American education will lack respectable national criteria, there will be no rites of passage, and anybody who wants to teach will be able to find a place regardless of his or her achievement records and instructional skills. I know this is true because I was named department chairman at St. Emeric's School in New York with no teaching experience and no education courses, and I know of teachers hired in other schools that don't even have a college degree. At St. Xavier High School, for example, one French teacher bragged that he never went to school beyond the sixth grade, and anyone who talked to him for more than twenty minutes knew he wasn't lying. He was finally discovered when his forged diploma arrived at the school and someone noticed he had misspelled Lehigh University.

More shocking, however, is the spelling of teachers for whom English isn't a second language. In a proposal for curriculum reform in Wales, Wisconsin, teachers, who didn't know or were too lazy to open a dictionary, wrote "dabate" for "debate," "documant" for "document," "woud" for "would," and "seperate" for "separate." My favorite spelling story is of a colleague who graduated from Arizona State, got a Master's degree in English from U.C.L.A., taught composition for almost three years at Ohio State, published in the *Denver Quarterly*, wrote film reviews for a national magazine, edited his own composition anthology, and was fired from a private high school because he couldn't spell. "But I wasn't hired to teach spelling," he protested.

Changing the ways in which we train our teachers is only half the problem, however. The other half is finding people who are qualified and willing to enter a profession in which there is little money, respect, or satisfaction. Ten years ago, twenty percent of the students entering college said they were interested in teaching; today the ratio is down to five percent and still dropping. By 1990, the supply of teachers will meet only eighty percent of the demand, less in math and science, where some states have already begun recruiting overseas.

Increasing the size and number of scholarships is one step toward attracting better students, especially if the grants are tied to a stipulation that the recipient teach one or two years for each year of financial aid. Not only are some of the less competitive students weeded out, but the chances of having a science teacher who believes a light year is about three minutes long will be greatly reduced.

Another way to improve the quality of tomorrow's educators is through "forgiveness loans," a practice initiated by Trinity University in San Antonio. Yearly grants of $5,000 to $6,000 are given to local high school students who graduate in the top ten percent of their class. If these students then teach for two years after they graduate from college, the loans are cancelled. Furthermore, the George W. Blackenridge Foundation, which provides the seed money for the project, will supplement the salaries of the graduates by $2,000 a year for each of the two years they teach.

Harvard University, meanwhile, is doing its share to improve the quality of education through its Mid-Career Math and Science Program, a one-year, $8,000 shot that provides education courses, teaching experience, and certification in thirty-three states.

A similar program is underway in New York City, which employs more than five hundred math teachers and two hundred science teachers who are not certified in their fields. Through an agreement between the Board of Education and thirteen of the city's metropolitan colleges, teachers who are certified in areas where there is a surplus and face unemployment can receive their full salary and teach only three periods a day if they take the required number of science and math courses to certify them in that field. Conversely, the final two periods are taught by science and math graduates who receive a $12,000 stipend as well as an introduction to public school teaching. Once a week, the teachers and graduates meet to exchange ideas and give advice.

The most immediate but most controversial approach to bringing qualified teachers into the schools is to bypass the certification requirements. New York City, which needs more than 4,000 new teachers, has begun hiring people with no teacher training but with bachelor's degrees and college credit-hours in certain education-related subjects. These new teachers will then have two years to complete the requirements for certification. The success of the program—more than 3,000 applications in one month—has inspired thirty-two states to consider similar measures.

Although many educators see these alternative routes as a good strategy for breaking down the certification procedures that have kept so many inferior schools of education in business, most teachers are against them. Their demands for more money, smaller classes, after-school compensation, and sabbaticals are frequently based on the idea that they are professionals, an idea conferred on them by the schools of education that have done so much to undermine teaching in the first place. Even though he can't speak highly of the country's teacher-training programs, Albert Shanker believes bypassing will do more harm than good because the new teachers' on-the-job training will be uncontrolled. Mary Futrell, head of the National Education Association, agrees: "It's a little scary to say we're now going to open up the profession to people who have not been trained."

It certainly is, Mary, but can they do much worse than those who have been "trained"? At least these new teachers will have expertise on their side, and in a profession that emphasizes skills more than knowledge, that's a big plus.

Here's why. Writing in the "Fall Education Survey" of 1984 for the New York Times, E.D. Hirsch tells of the time his son, who teaches in a high school, mentioned in one of his classes that Latin isn't spoken anymore. "But what about in Latin America?" asked one disbelieving student. Perhaps a high school student might be forgiven for lacking the kind of information that Hirsch's son may have taken for granted, but what about a college student? At the City University of New York, I had students who didn't know whether Boston was a city or a state and only one in a class of twenty five had ever heard of Ulysses S. Grant and Robert E. Lee. She thought they "might be generals." In a graduate seminar at Ohio State University—a school whose former President wanted it to be a place the football team could be proud of—not one of eighteen students knew of the Berlin Wall.

Many educators don't see anything wrong with this kind of cultural illiteracy. Students of skills and later teachers of skills, they regard reading ability as something that enables us to acquire whatever specific information we will someday need. It's not much different from hitting a baseball. Reading may not be as easy as swinging a bat or as dependent on hand-eye coordination, but it is a skill that can be coached and developed.

This is true in the earlier grades when pupils are being taught elementary phonics and how to identify words, says Hirsch, but "it becomes an oversimplification when students start reading for meaning rather than for cracking the alphabetic code. If reading *were* just hitting the right alphabetic ball with the right phonic bat, or just learning 'text strategies,' it *would* be like baseball. We could teach everybody to groove his swings, and watch for the seven types of pitches."

The trouble with reading is that the rules are as variable as the subjects and their authors, so that as we mature as readers our ability depends less on our skills and more on the information we've accumulated. At a college in Richmond, Virginia, Hirsch found that the students there knew as little about Grant and Lee as mine did in New York, but they performed as well as highly educated readers on a text about friendships. There was nothing wrong with their reading skills, just their range of knowledge. If the current crop of teachers entering our schools without any method training can help narrow the information gap so painfully described by Hirsch, they may do much to improve their students' learning abilities as well as contribute to a life that depends so heavily on the information we share.

Raising teachers' salaries, improving their working conditions, and restoring respect to the profession through tougher admission, course, and graduation requirements in our schools of education can't help but bring better people into the profession. So will competency testing, increasing the size and number of scholarships, establishing more "forgiveness" loans, creating financial incentives for successful teachers, weeding out the unproductive, and permitting the knowledgeable to bypass the rigid certification requirements that serve to keep so many education departments in business.

Perhaps the best way to rebuild the profession's reputation, however, is to restore its sense of idealism. By viewing their careers as a calling and nurturing the missionary zeal that is so often at the root of good teaching, teachers can place themselves on a level above that of the materialists who scorn them, learn to respect themselves for the people they are and the work they do, and serve their students' best interests without sacrificing their own integrity.

IV
THE UPPER DECKS

Less than a year before he was to be banned from speaking at Harvard College, Ralph Waldo Emerson delivered the school's Phi Beta Kappa address on the state of American scholarship. Known today as "The American Scholar," Emerson's speech declared the American mind to be free from its authoritative European heritage. It proclaimed not our scholars' accomplishments (there weren't many) but rather discussed the problems that came from following established models too closely. "The American Scholar" also defined what Emerson thought a scholar should be—not a "mere thinker" or "the parrot of other men's thinking," but MAN THINKING, a creative, concrete thinker who is actively engaged in solving the problems of human existence.

Is the American scholar of today MAN THINKING? Is he a vital, energetic force moving minds toward important issues? The answer is all too clear. By limiting the rewards of academic life mostly to research and publication, much of which is unimaginative and premature, American universities are chaneling their young scholars' energies into writing mostly irrelevant books for superiors who are not interested in judging their work with people.

Because the scope of scholarship is limited mostly to factual research with publication as the major determining factor for academic success, today's young scholars confront a tyrant not much different in nature from the European authorities Emerson had to deal with. Both models present a criterion for judgment that eliminates those intangibles of art that can be approached but never controlled by factual research, namely, imagination and philosophy. Consequently, as Emerson pointed out, "Young men of the fairest promise . . . are hindered from action by the principles on which business is managed, and turn drudges, or die of disgust, some of them suicides."

In her book, *Orlando*, Virginia Woolf tells the story of a party at which the conversation of the guests is deadening. Because of their high opinion of themselves, however, the guests are enchanted by what they believe to be their own and each other's wit. When Alexander Pope arrives, he makes three originally witty remarks which the guests can neither understand nor respond to. The party is ruined. Mrs. Woolf then explains that one such saying was bad enough, but no society could survive three of them. No limited society can survive originality because originality does not observe all the rules of the game. The state of American scholarship today is not much different from the party in *Orlando*. It continues to be predictable. Today's scholars continue to do and say what their accepted models did and said. The only time originality is tolerated is when it is harmless, when it doesn't threaten the status quo.

Any graduate student writing a term paper knows that there must be no question of spoiling the party. Intelligence is warmly appreciated as long as it is presented in the proper form. This widespread emphasis in today's universities on *how* something is said rather than on *what* is said frequently encourages students to pen sentences like: "Had the protagonist known beforehand that guppies lack a hypothalomus structure and can consequently be overfed, Raymond's love for his father's fish would not have resulted in their demise." Doing their best to sound as close as they can to the models that have been established for them, today's graduate students often write sentences that border on the unintelligible: "Irregardless of the fact that the protagonist's ignorance, then, is the root cause of the disproportion which exists between his good intentions (saving his friend's life) and the reality those intentions encounter (failure, old age, and his father's death), the disproportion between the two enables the protagonist to be both innocent and guilty at the same time."

By never quite crossing the threshold of intelligibility and by disguising their position with careful footnotes, annotated bibliographies, and all the other apparatuses of intelligentsia, today's graduate students continue to assure the guardians of scholarship that they are harmless. Furthermore, as long as our young scholars continued to exchange their principles and ideals (assuming they have any left) for the disproportionate pressures of academic advancement, American universities will continue to produce what Emerson calls "The book-learned class, who value books as such, not as related to nature and the human condition ... Hence the restorers of readings, the emendators, the bibliomaniacs of all degrees."

Of course, there are exceptions. Richard McCann from the University of Iowa dropped his dissertation on Joan Didion to write one that focused on his own poetry. Fortunately, his mentors in the Creative Writing Department recognized the worth of Richard's new dissertation proposal and encouraged him to discover his place in the context of modern American literature. Unfortunately, his "non-traditional" degree now hinders his finding a job. What department wants to take on a beginning assistant professor who's already good enough to be the subject of a dissertation? What department chairman needs someone who's had a book of poems published, was a writer-in-residence at the Fine Arts Work Center in Provincetown and the Virginia Center for the Arts, and served as a Fulbright Professor at the University of Göteborg in Sweden before he even had his doctorate? Most of the chairmen I've known have never written anything creative or at least never had it published, may have edited an anthology somewhere in their careers, probably published an article or two in a magazine no one ever reads, and have almost certainly never traveled out of the country except on vacation—which is why they're department chairmen. Having failed to be MEN THINKING, they don't need someone like Richard McCann around to make them look worse than they already are.

But we're talking about scholars here, not department chairmen, and how they've separated themselves from the trunk of humanity by creating their own class of restorers, emendators, and bibliomaniacs. Like scientists, they've gone into the laboratory and learned scientific methods, but unlike the scientists, the scholars have rarely come out.

Scientists measure fact. They observe, experiment, discover, and record for purposes that will affect humanity. Generally speaking, science has been successful in providing man with the means necessary to control his environment and, when engaged in the pursuit of responsible goals, science makes significant contributions to man's welfare. Art, on the other hand, has always been beyond science, though not reason. Its basic substance has never been dates, circumstances, sources, and reference.

The scientific scholar has been able to demonstrate that facts are important for a more meaningful understanding of a given work, but he has also misled those interested in art into believing they know what they may well not understand. For example, where an artist gets his material is not as important as what he does with it. The quality of Shakespeare's art cannot be attributed to Holinshed's *Chronicles*. Hence, the fact that Shakespeare got a lot of his plots from Holinshed is only of incidental interest, and yet, there are more than a few graduate students who seek out courses featuring writers who used Holinshed as one of their sources. Every semester they write essentially the same paper; only the play and the plot change.

Factual research is important—no one is denying that—but its importance must not be overemphasized. When it is, the effect can be deadening, if not downright dull. I had a student at the City University of New York who believed that every page of a term paper had to have at least five footnotes. Can you imagine writing one? What must it have been like trying to squeeze five footnotes in on every page? How many times did she get to the bottom of a page with only four? Never had I read a paper with more erasures than words, and never had this unfortunate student ever been told that art—the portrayal of people, imagination, and ideas—is an expression of life and can no more be fully explained by its facts than life itself can.

By basing their policies upon theories of limited application, scholars have eliminated unsupported rhetoric and insufficient generalizations, but they have also thrown aside intuition for experiment and discovery for interpretation.

People like Matthew Arnold will no longer be able to get away with writing treatises on Celtic literature without knowing a word of Celtic, but there will also be fewer Matthew Arnolds. Scholars have wisely gone into the laboratory for aid, and art has benefited from science's help, but most scholars in America are still in the laboratory establishing standards that are influencing the next generation to pin down all of art to an area of thought that falls far short of encompassing all of art.

Conversely, Emerson's MEN THINKING, as few of them as there may be, know that true scholarship means more than being a technician. They know that *real* intellectual pursuits cannot be reduced to the specialized roles that academic society assigns. Real scholarship, like art, is more than a matter of systems, organizations, and structures. It is a matter of people who encounter, respect, and speak to one another about life and who, despite disagreement, also listen.

1. Getting Your Papers

It is not unusual to find people where you work who are unwilling to listen, but in academia, even speaking is discouraged. I was told by at least two senior faculty members at Boston University that if I planned to stay around for more than just a few semesters, I had best be seen and not heard, regardless of how trivial the subject or how much I happened to know about it.

Of all the people I know who received their Ph.D.'s when I did or since, only one has been granted tenure. And the secret of his success? "On the very first day I left for my first class, I asked my wife if she had any advice to offer on my working in my third college in seven years. 'This time,' she said, 'keep your mouth shut.' I did, and it worked. I never volunteered a view on anything and, if asked my opinion of anything anybody else said, I always said I thought the idea had its merits and should be considered. For years I said nothing but that. 'The idea has its merits and should be considered.' I could have been a robot. 'Joe's idea is a good one; I think we should talk about it.' *They* thought I was a genius. *Everyone* loved me."

Why anyone would want to work in this kind of environment, I can't begin to say. Perhaps they still hold on to some ideal of what it means to be a teacher. Perhaps, like me, that ideal is combined with the reality of having not been wanted on the lower levels of education. But higher does not necessarily mean better. I mentioned in an earlier chapter my being fired from St. Xavier High School for writing a letter protesting the treatment of another teacher, but how about the time I lost my graduate assistantship at New York University for displaying what I thought was a sense of humor?

I had never liked Professor Baudin, an incompetent teacher who hadn't published spit, rode into the department on his father's coattails, and was put in charge of the graduate assistants because he couldn't stand being in the classroom anymore. Graduate assistants are students who work on their doctorates and cut down on their education expenses at the same time by teaching two composition courses each semester in exchange for two free courses and a small stipend. Mine was $215 a month. The only criterion for an assistantship is an M.A. degree and enrollment in the doctoral program, but Prof. Baudin also looked for people who were married and whose spouses could support them. He had had trouble in the past with people who actually tried to live on their stipends.

Well, I was divorced by then, but I desperately needed the assistantship because a Ph.D. isn't enough to land a teaching job. You also need college teaching experience. So planning to have three days a week to substitute teach in the city's public schools, I lied.

What I hadn't planned on, of course, was my classes being scheduled over four days instead of two, leaving one day free—the very day Prof. Baudin chose to hold his weekly meeting with the graduate assistants. I went to the first meeting and learned how to correct any composition in less than five minutes: Only read the first and last paragraphs and one paragraph in between. Another tip—if you believe some student suspects you of not reading her whole paper—

is to throw out the third page of her next paper. When the student then asks you for the missing page, you say you must have lost it while correcting it.

In the second meeting I learned how to justify a "C" grade regardless of the quality of the paper. That was the last meeting I attended but not for noble reasons. I had run out of money. My first check from N.Y.U. was two weeks away, and I had yet to earn any money from teaching.

The next Wednesday and the Wednesday after that I substitute taught. By the Wednesday after that I had fallen out of favor with Prof. Baudin. I had also fallen out of favor with myself by jumping every turnstile that stood in my way and stealing from a Key Food in Brooklyn everything I put into my mouth for weeks.

I was still a week shy of my first substitution check—the assistantship money having gone to rent and electricity—when I got caught by the store detective. Tired of lying and stealing and running, I told the store manager what I had been doing and why. He told me to keep the bar of soap and wedge of cheese I had stuffed into my pockets. He wasn't going to have me arrested; he was going to give me ten dollars. But if he saw my fucking face in his store ever again, he'd beat the living shit out of me.

The next day, I found myself walking behind Prof. Baudin on my way to school. I remember wanting to tell him that Key Food had more compassion in one little store in Brooklyn than New York University had in all of Washington Square, but he had been sending me more than a few memos demanding to know why I had stopped coming to his Wednesday meetings, so I tried to keep myself from overtaking him. Every time he looked in a store window, I did also. This went on for several blocks until, crossing University Place, Prof. Baudin put his finger to his nose and blew its contents into the street. Not having spent much time in the South, I had never seen anybody litter this way. Nor, I imagine, had Prof. Baudin ever seen anybody watch him do it. Trying to keep the conversation light, I told him that now I knew what Whitman meant when he said the grass was the Lord's handkerchief.

Baudin wasn't impressed. "You just lost your assistantship, son, but I'm glad to see you've learned something here." Of course there were other reasons for firing me, obvious ones, but to this day I can't get over the weight of the given one. Why would people want to enter a profession where there is such a surplus of people that they can be dismissed so easily? The only answer I can come up with is that they must genuinely love literature. Or pain. Either way, they had better have a strong commitment to the former and a high tolerance for the latter if they hope to survive.

And surviving doesn't mean getting tenure. Surviving means being one of the forty percent of all people who have received their Ph.D.'s in language and literature since 1970 who will not have to give up teaching. Surviving means being one of the forty-two percent of that group to land a job leading to tenure and then managing to be one of the forty-two percent of that group to actually get tenure — if they're lucky.

A lot of theorists claim that sixty percent of that number will be forced to leave the profession after at least six years of full-time teaching in tenure track positions. In other words, if you've just won your Ph.D. in language or literature, your chances of surviving the *Titanic* would have been better than getting tenure now.

And don't think this has made department chairmen any kinder or more sympathetic. They know they're in a buyer's market, and a lot of them are enjoying every minute of it. Several months ago, I went to the annual Modern Language Association Convention to be interviewed for positions opening up in nine months. At the first interview I was asked five questions by a panel of five professors:

Who is the Great Brown God?

What twentieth-century writer wrote a sequel to a novel he published early in his career?

Who is the most important character in Ernest Hemingway's *The Sun Also Rises*?

What is your philosophy of composition?

What will you contribute to our school outside of the classroom?

I knew the answers to the first two, the Mississippi and John

Updike, but the most important character in *The Sun Also Rises*, I was told, was not Jake or Brett or Cohn or even the matador but the *landscape*!

I decided I didn't want to teach at this school, so I admitted having no philosophy of composition and claimed my major contribution to the college would be to provide entertaining conversation at parties and receptions. The panel thought this was brilliant and very funny and just what they needed. Several weeks later, they offered me the job.

One college not to offer me a position was Indianapolis University in Indiana. Its representative had suggested I call her when I got to the conference, which is usually not a difficult task in spite of her not knowing what hotel she would be in or that no hotel releases the room number of any interviewer for fear of unleashing a flood of phone calls by job seekers. The way to contact an interviewer at the M.L.A. is through a special service which will give you a room number providing your name is on a previously submitted list. The problem in my case was that I.U.'s representative hadn't submitted any list of names, only the name of the hotel where she was staying, which of course was under orders not to release the room numbers.

Well, it took me almost two hours to find a hotel employee who was young enough, naive enough, kind enough, and pliable enough to give me the number and, when I finally got through on the telephone, the interviewer told me to come to her room right away. I rushed from the lobby to the fourth floor and rang the bell. "Hi, I'm Richard Andersen. I just spoke to you . . . "

"You're late, but you might as well come in. The person I should be interviewing hasn't shown up yet."

I explain that the person she's expecting may be having trouble locating her. "Your name isn't listed with the 'Who's Where' service; I had a terrible time getting through."

She tells me she purposely makes herself difficult to contact in order to test the sincerity of the candidates.

I know by now that I don't want to work at Indianapolis University either, but what if none of the other schools I've applied to offer me a job? I can't leave, but staying means listening to the interviewer complain about two men in her department who consistently receive high evaluations from their students. She's convinced it's because of their deep voices, which she says makes them seem more knowledgeable and authoritative than women.

When I arrive home, there's a letter waiting for me which says I'm the new James Thurber Writer-in-Residence at Ohio State University. For one year, I get to live rent-free in Thurber's old home in Columbus, a stipend of $25,000 – as opposed to the $19,000 the lucky winner of the assistant professor competition will get – and write, write, write.

Why, you may ask, can the winner of an international writer's competition not find a better university to interview him for a job than one in which the best teachers are discredited because of their deep voices? The answer is simple: unless you are a nationally renowned scholar who will bring money and prestige to a college or a recent Ph.D. with no publications, little or no teaching experience, and, most importantly, no indication of any potential, you are out of luck. People with accomplishments and promise can't find a job because they won't be easy to get rid of when the time comes to replace them with cheaper help.

When I was hired at the College of Basic Studies, I thought I was the best of the four hundred candidates who had applied. I was thirty years old, had over five years of high school teaching experience as well as two semesters of college teaching experience, and, like Walt Whitman, I had tried to develop "a good head rather than a full one" by teaching in as many different kinds of schools as I could find, living or at least traveling in as many different countries as I could afford, and working in as many different kinds of jobs as I could qualify for. By the time I moved to Boston, I had taught on the elementary, secondary, and college levels in public, private, parochial, and military settings with all black, all white, all Hispanic, all boys, all girls, and coed students. I had lived in New York, California, Colorado, and France, crossed the United States at least twenty times, and toured every country between Ireland and Turkey. I had worked as everything from a teacher and director of an international cultural exchange program to a dishwasher, carpet loomer, bicycle messenger, door-to-door salesman, factory laborer, and ditchdigger. Within a week I once went from the third ranking officer on the second largest class ship in the United States Navy to a garbageman making $17-a-day on New York's Floating Hospital. Who could possibly have been better than me?

Everybody. Looking through the rejected applications just before they were to be thrown out, I noticed hundreds of people from better schools with more interesting dissertation topics, more varied college teaching experience, and, yes, even publications in magazines like *PMLA*, *Spectrum*, and *The New York Review of Books*. I had at the time one publication: a review of the movie *Marathon Man* that was printed by a Zionist newspaper because the screenplay happened to be by someone whose last name is Goldman.

When the department chairman read my application, he saw a high school teacher who got his Ph.D. relatively late and wasn't going anywhere. Much the same can be said for the three people hired with me: a Ph.D. from Brandeis who still worked as an advisor in his old dormitory because he didn't publish enough to earn the rank he needed to support his wife and two children, an M.A. from Indiana who had been teaching full-time for seven years but had yet to complete his dissertation, and a band manager for whom teaching helped pay the rent until the real money started rolling in. The only candidate who was worse than us, so I was told, was a minority applicant from a guilt-ridden college who didn't know George Eliot was a woman and thought British spellings were typographical errors.

2. The Floating Bottom

The Floating Bottom is as solid a fixture in most colleges as any academic department: A pool of young, untenured, mostly inexperienced instructors whose job it is to teach the lowest levels of classes to the worst students for the least pay and then be replaced just before they start thinking seriously about tenure. At the College of Basic Studies, the band leader lasted two years, the residence hall advisor and I were fired after three, and the M.A. veteran of Floating Bottoms at Indiana and William and Mary, quit teaching altogether. Unfortunately but predictably, he knew, loved, and taught literature better than any of us.

The great advantage of a Floating Bottom—for administrators, that is—is that the inexperienced don't know they're in one until it's too late. You hear about it, but you don't believe it really exists—at least not in your school. Like so many children in a garden of the Fitzi-Contini, you convince yourself that those on their way out are bitter because they didn't make the grade, you believe your chairman when he labels them "malcontents" or "misanthropes," you remember that the job advertisement said "tenure-track" and, though you learn no one has gotten tenure at the college in years, you know there's still a chance for you because that last lucky person didn't score particularly high on his student's evaluations and he never published so much as a single word. Granting tenure to such a blatant mediocrity was one of the wisest moves the College of Basic Studies ever made. It gave hope to everyone who will ever come after him.

The Floating Bottom also benefits the students, who are probably more inclined to learn from the young, energetic, eager-to-succeed crop of teachers who burn themselves out so their superiors in the department can have more time to do less work on the increased salaries they receive at the expense of the poorly paid junior faculty.

It was the "malcontents" at the College of Basic Studies who forwarded to the dean and faculty-at-large a letter citing some of the reasons for their low morale:

> Salaries for junior faculty are among the lowest for faculty in the entire nation.
>
> One year contracts mean that junior faculty must spend every fall looking for another job.
>
> Tenure appointments tend to be arbitrary. At the College of Basic Studies, which has had one ap-

pointment in seven years, it appears tenure is an impossibility.

On many occasions, junior faculty appear not to be treated with the respect and dignity that college faculty members should receive. Authoritarian nuances and intimidation ("if you want to stay, don't make waves") cannot substitute for trust and confidence in promoting faculty commitment.

Other significant points include lack of substantive input into the curriculum and the uses to which faculty evaluations are put.

Some places, like the City University of New York, have created a Floating Middle, a small group of untenured faculty whose tenuous position is pressured from beneath by an ever increasing pool of part-time instructors. These adjuncts, as they are called, save the university hundreds of thousands of dollars in health insurance, retirement benefits, promotions, salary increments, office expenses, travel funds, leaves of absence, even wages. Not only do adjunct professors come cheap (from $1,000 for a thirteen week course at a small private college like Marymount Manhattan to $1,800 a course at the City University), any three of them can do the work of two full-time professors at half the cost.

But do they do it as well? Unfortunately, for the thousands of students who are so frequently made to suffer first and most, the answer is no. In education, as in so many things in life, you get what you pay for. Knowing they are heavily exploited in a buyer's market, many adjuncts make it their policy *not* to hold office hours, work at registration, accept committee assignments, attend faculty meetings, or counsel their students outside of the classroom. Others take off every minute for which they can still be paid (usually one hour per semester for each hour they teach in a week) to work on books, stories, poems, screenplays, job applications—anything that will get them out of the adjunct pool and into the Floating Bottom, where at least they'll make *some* money, use their medical plans to see a doctor, get their teeth fixed if they budget carefully, and have their shot at the tenure that doesn't exist any longer—unless, of course, the school is so bad or in such a poor location that tenure is its only draw.

Although some adjuncts can add significant dimensions to any department, most are clearly temporary help. Hired to save money and often at the last minute with only a hasty review of their credentials, adjuncts receive little recognition or respect.

At the City University of New York, there's a well-known story about a night adjunct who dropped by his department during the day to check his mailbox. The telephone rang and, since the secretary wasn't there, he answered it. Meanwhile, the chairperson, who had met the adjunct but didn't remember him from any of the other seventy temporaries she had hired, came in from her classes, went straight to her office, and called the police.

The police came and the adjunct explained who he was, but there was no record in the department of either him or his classes. The adjunct pointed to his name on the mailbox—an old trick according to the police—and lacking any other identification—he was on his way to play basketball—he was taken to the nearest precinct until the following night when twenty students flooded the English Department, wanting to know if their class had been cancelled.

With treatment like this, is it any wonder why so many adjuncts try to get as much out of their colleges as their colleges are trying to get out of them? And I'm not talking just about stealing paper clips or using the photocopy machine to copy their own manuscripts. I know at least a dozen adjuncts at two colleges within the same university who request each other as substitute teachers the same week they both take off every semester, thus enabling them to double their paychecks for that week. It only comes to an extra $200 a semester for each of them, but when you're counting pennies as they are, $200 can make a real difference. The adjuncts' general lack of commitment also throws an inordinate amount of advising and paper work on the full-time faculty and, when you consider most adjuncts teach composition and basic introductory courses, it doesn't take much imagination to realize that in their efforts to save a buck, our colleges are undermining the quality of education on one of its most important levels.

Teachers have been complaining about the Floating Bottom and the over-use of adjuncts for years (65 out of 90 teachers in the English Deparment at Manhattan Community College and 10,000 out of 24,000 in the State University of New York are adjuncts), but has anyone ever listened? Yes, in 1979, the tenured faculty at Boston University was at bitter odds with its president, John Silber, over whether teachers could form themselves into an industrial-style union and bargain collectively. Silber insisted that professors were not an industrial workforce but a component of management. The faculty said it was Silber's not including them in management decisions that drove them to the union in the first place. It was a nasty fight with the tenured faculty trying to get all the support they could from the untenured teachers, the clerical staff, the librarians, the maintenance workers, and the security police, while Silber paid more than $250,000 from his tuition-dependent university to Modern Management Methods, a union-busting consulting firm that the *New Republic* described as the modern legal and psychological equivalent of the "company thugs" and "state militia" of the nineteenth century.

Things went from bad to worse, but in the fall of 1979, the tenured faculty needed help, and for the first time in a long time were willing not only to listen but also to promise whatever was necessary to swell the ranks of their union. Because most of the junior faculty hadn't been around when the conflict began in 1974, received the greater part of their information from the senior faculty, and wanted to please these first barriers to tenure and happiness, they supported the union in exchange for a promise to raise their salaries above the "insult" Silber had offered and work out an agreeable solution to their other problems as well.

The strike came when Silber refused to sign the contract his negotiators had agreed to. The union cried foul, but so did the junior faculty. Silber's original "insult," it was revealed, contained a greater increase in salary than the contract approved by the faculty union. The younger teachers had been betrayed! Push came to shove within the ranks, and that's when the tenured teachers showed their true colors; any junior faculty member who was not on that picket line wouldn't have to worry about tenure because he'd be out of a job. But that wasn't the worst thing they did. When a contract was finally ratified after nine days of striking, the union went back into the classroom with the librarians and clerical workers still out on the street.

Although the union's methods only aggravated the conflict between senior and junior faculty, Boston University's problems with its Floating Bottom are not much different from those of other universities with their adjuncts. Some schools, such as the University of Massachusetts at Amherst, have avoided the Floating Bottom and adjunct pool by awarding more graduate assistantships. But with the number of graduate assistants (1,500), now exceeding the number of faculty (1,300), U. Mass. finds itself wrestling with many of the same problems as Boston University and the City University of New York: the graduate assistants, many of whom are undertrained and undereducated, have begun to feel undernourished—they make $5,200 a year plus tuition for two courses—and their students are beginning to complain that they don't get to see a "real" professor until their junior year.

As government cutbacks and the decline in enrollment meshes with the increase in underemployed Ph.D.'s and our colleges' willingness to become more and more exploitative, the techniques and attitudes of industry will continue to come into conflict with traditional views of what a university means.

3. The View From the Bridge

On December 18, 1979, the largest faculty assembly in Boston University's history voted 457 to 215 to urge the dismissal of the president, John Silber. It was the teachers' second vote of no confidence in Silber in four years. Six years later Silber was one of two candidates being considered to replace T.H. Bell, the retiring Secretary of Education. How he descended into the ashes of 1979 and then rose from them like a phoenix to join Henry Kissinger's Commission on Latin America, become a leading panelist on the National Endowment for the Humanities' study on the state of education, and play an important role in President Reagan's educational reform movement, is a testament to his management of Boston University and a good metaphor for meassuring the management systems of our country's other colleges.

Boston University isn't Harvard, but it isn't Miami Dade either. The fourth largest private university in the United States, B.U. (where one and one is two, its detractors like to say) had a solid second-rate reputation until Nora Ephron (*Esquire*, September 1977) helped put it and its petulant president on the map with a scathing attack on its management methods. Nevertheless, Silber came out the victor, and Boston University is now touted as a model for other schools to follow whenever the question arises as to whether economically sound management is compatible with traditional academia.

The son of a frequently unemployed architect, John Robert Silber was born in San Antonio in 1926 without his right forearm. An embryonic but usable hand juts out from just below his elbow. In her article for *Esquire*, Ephron insensitively suggests that Silbur's handicap is the root cause of many of his problems, most notably, an overcompensating defensiveness and an almost uncontrolled desire for power. Silber, for his part, claims that after he was twelve years old nobody said a thing about his arm until he arrived in Boston.

Silber graduated *summa cum laude* from Trinity University in San Antonio and took his doctorate in philosophy from Yale in 1956. He started his teaching career at Yale but didn't make a name for himself in academia until he became Dean of the College of Arts and Sciences at the University of Texas, where he emerged as a crack disputationist and, ironically, a defender of faculty rights, and the principle of collegiality – a loose word that covers everything from getting along with one another to a share for everyone in governance.

When he came to Boston University in 1971, Silber saw that under its surface reputation, B.U. had the faculty and potential to become an academic leader. One of the first steps he took was to raise by $8,000 the yearly salary of Helen Vendler, an internationally renowned scholar who had just been offered a competitive contract by Yale. It is typical of Silber's behavior, however (not to mention an example of the pettiness which exists on even the highest levels of education), that when Vendler opposed his stand on unionization, he interpreted her criticism as an attempt to show her colleagues she wasn't in anybody's pocket.

In addition to holding on to the university's best professors, Silber was given the Herculean order of balancing the school's budget, improving its fund-raising capabilities, building up its endowment, widening its national visibility, and increasing its enrollment.

He did it all and more. Boston University's entering classes, in a reversal of the national trend, have scored higher and higher on their Scholastic Aptitude Tests. Its faculty now includes such heavyweights as John Findlay (philosophy), Sigmund Koch (psychology), George Starbuck (creative writing), and the recipient of the 1986 Nobel Peace Prize, Eve Wiesel. The school's programs in health, education, economics, and archeology are now conducted in more than fifty foreign countries. Even the famous Olympic hockey team that upset the Soviet Union at Lake Placid had four players from Boston University.

Almost singlehandedly, Silber has balanced the budget without drawing on the university's reserves, centralized and brought order to the budget-setting process, increased the amount of federally funded research (one of these projects winning Senator Proxmire's Golden Fleece Award for wasting taxpayers' money), gained national recognition for himself through his concept of a Tuition Advance Fund that enables needy students to borrow tuition from the government and repay it later as a percentage of personal income), created over two hundred new faculty positions, and turned into the most popular second choice among all graduating high school seniors a university few people had ever heard about outside of New England and the Jewish community surrounding New York City.

Nevertheless, many of Silber's colleagues in Boston and throughout the county see his reign as a strip-mining operation that has deeply scarred academic life and has set into motion a national policy that will irreparably destroy the ecology of teaching, scholarship, learning, and service to the community.

One of those rare individuals who's learned that success is based on property, wealth, *and* political power, Silber has announced plans for a joint building venture with the City of Boston that includes malls, shops, hotels, subways, and a skyscraper. Which wouldn't be so bad if Boston University weren't such a lousy landlord. In spite of an outraged protest by local residents, the administration forcibly evicted an elderly couple, one of them bedridden, from the apartment they'd lived in for most of their lives. Only after a state representative intervened and it looked as if the story might spread beyond Boston did the university relent. Sort of. It promised not to throw the old people out until their lease expired.

But property acquisition is not the only means by which Silber assures his university's growth. Another policy is to admit children of the wealthy in exchange for financial support. Transcripts from a meeting of the University Needs Committee quotes Silber as saying, "There have been any number of people crawling all over me for admission to our medical school and our law school who have never been tapped systematically for a gift to this university, and I'm not ashamed to sell those indulgences."

Later in the meeting, an honorary trustee by the name of Louis Rosenfeld told Silber, "John, I'm very happy you've cleared my conscience because when I got this boy into the law school and I demanded $50,000, I was greatly criticized." When asked by a reporter from the *Village Voice* to explain his policy of selling admissions, Silber claimed that anybody with any wit could understand that the people conversing on the transcript were joking.

Probing potential benefactors is a part of any school's fundraising mechanism, but Boston University's list includes detailed profiles—some laced with embarrassing gossip—on hundreds of unsuspecting people. F. Lee Bailey's file, for example, notes his censure by the Massachusetts bar and concludes that the famous alumnus spends his money "as fast as he earns it and therefore obtaining a substantial gift from him may prove to be difficult." The height and weight of another prospect—five feet five and 138 pounds—is listed after an apparent rival in his field tells an investigator, "He may be rich and powerful, but he will always be short." These files, along with the university's "Widows Program" and "Necrology List," could be written off as merely amusing if they didn't also reveal some questionable practices. Like the time the university awarded a lucrative contract to one of its own trustees in exchange for a donation, or when an honorary trustee who was expected to bequeath the university a million dollars received pre-admission for his grandchildren in the twenty-first century. Rather than question the impropriety or possible illegality of the university's methods, however, Silber maintains that they are the perfectly routine procedures of any competently run institution.

Perhaps they are. So too perhaps are the methods Silber employed to prevent any labor organizing on campus. The first serious drive for a union began in 1975 among the secretaries at the College of Liberal Arts. Soon, however, the campaign blossomed into a full-scale effort to enlist all the clerical workers. Leading the campaign were Liz Hirsh and Patti Schiffer, two employees of the university's health clinic, which happened to be run by Wilbur Hemperly, the husband of Silber's personal secretary whom he brought with him from Texas.

Hemperly fired the women in 1975 after they had protested working conditions at the clinic. The women appealed to the National Labor Relations Board, which after a year-long investigation, found the firings unlawful and ordered B.U. to rehire the workers. Three months later, the women were fired again, and though no reason was given for their dismissal, Hirsh and Schiffer charged that Hemperly had built a cubicle around them to isolate them from the other workers, tripled their work load, demoted them, and abused them verbally. The N.L.R.B. investigated the second firing and on

May 4, 1978, authorized contempt of court proceedings to begin against Boston University. Less than a month later, the Silber administration agreed to pay the women $101,500. Why? To avoid rehiring them? That's what the university wanted people to believe. The real reason, according to Hirsh's husband, was a personal damages suit that Hirsh and Schiffer had drawn up against B.U. on the testimony of a fellow worker who overheard Hemperly trying to get a contract on the women's lives.

Labor battles have never been easily won at Boston University and victories for the unions have never lasted long. Like the secretaries, the faculty had to go in and out of court and on and off the picket line before they got their contract, and even then Silber found an excuse to try to fire five active union members for engaging in a sympathy strike with the clerical workers and librarians that the teachers had left on the picket line while they marched back into their classrooms.

The action prompted academic pandemonium. Six hundred students marched in protest, 3,000 faculty from colleges across the country signed petitions demanding the five professors' reinstatement, and the B.U. faculty voted for the second time in three years to urge Silber's dismissal.

At the same time, the Civil Liberties Union of Massachusetts concluded that the university had violated the principles of academic freedom and free speech by, among other things, cutting funds to the student newspaper for daring to pose the editorial question, "Has Silber Gone Too Far?" Other publications critical of Silber—*Commonwealth*, *Rising River*, *Women's Yellow Pages*, *Urthona*, *Blackfold*, *Comment*, and *Commentaries*—also bit the dust. And if things weren't bad enough, the Massachusetts Board of Medicine announced it was investigating charges of malpractice at the health clinic.

In times of controversy, however, none of Silber's considerable skills are more apparent than his ability as a rhetorician. In an interview on *60 Minutes*, he scored a tremendous national triumph by projecting himself as a tough, angry, unfairly persecuted leader. He explained, and not without justification, that much of the faculty's discontent was the result of having their light eclipsed by the several dozen brighter luminaries he had brought in. Before he became president, Silber claimed, many of the faculty were second-raters who, in the absence of first-rate people, had passed themselves off as the best in their fields. By recruiting as many outstanding writers and scholars as he had, however, Silber changed the ambience of mediocrity. Of course they resented him! They also resented John Barth and William Arrowsmith, who, among others, had to leave the university because they felt ostracized.

Silber also let his detractors and the nation know that a university shouldn't be confused with a democracy. A university is not a government in that sense; therefore, his administration was not accountable to the faculty and students but to the trustees. Not only that but some of his responsibilities, such as balancing the budget, were not subjects on which the faculty had any substantial experience or any great contributions to make.

Which didn't mean the teachers weren't managers, however. Writing an *amicus* for the Supreme Court in his support of Yeshiva University's attempt to prevent faculty unions on the grounds that professors aren't workers, Silber wrote: "Thus the faculty as managers select the raw materials (i.e. the students), design the manufacturing process (i.e. the curriculum to develop the educated student), manufacture the product (i.e. give grades to the students), and, if satisfied, recommend the product (i.e. the student) for sale (i.e. for graduation as a holder of degree)."

And as for censoring the students' publications, Silber wasn't about to give anybody money which the university was accountable for and then let them spend it anyway they wanted without a review by the administration on how the money should be spent.

This may sound good to those who believe that rigidity and bombast are a workable response to a world of endless complexity and frequent frustration—perhaps that was Silber's appeal to the Reagan administration—but a university needs managers who also have an *educational* vision. Silber has a vision, and no one can deny he's brought the university's medical, allied medical, and dental schools as well as its music, fine arts, history, English, philosophy, developmental economics, and clinical psychology departments to heights they've never known. However, the question still exists as to whether Silber's *educational* vision has not been impaired by a controlled, economic, product-oriented management system that has undermined what many universities consider their major asset—the morale, good will, and creative contributions of the academic community.

That the trustees don't think it has may be gleaned, according to one ex-trustee, from the almost ritualistic vote of support for President Silber that closes many of their meetings and their occasional wrapping of him in an American flag. The image of Silber draped in red, white, and blue could not be more appropriate for a board led by chairman Arthur Metcalf, head of the Electronics Corporation of America. A member of the right-wing Freedom Foundation at Valley Forge and board chairman of the United Strategic Institute, a think-tank for conservative and military intellectuals, Metcalf has written: "The dilemma in which the professional military in the United States presently finds itself has come to resemble that in the Third Reich under the Nazi regime when the professional duty to obey the political leadership— amateurs in military matters—was unreconcilable with the professional responsibility for the security of the Nation."

As long as wealthy, defense minded Republicans run this country, there'll be no threat of a coup from Arthur Metcalf. The same holds true for one of the country's microcosms, Boston University. Speaking in military phrases, Silber has claimed that Berkeley was the "distant warning line" of higher education in the Sixties, and Boston University is the "DEW Line of the Eighties."

He's probably right. Not only that but he's probably not as far out of line as his detractors would like us to believe. The acquisition of property, the bought admissions, the fabulous fund raising schemes, the union busting, even the censoring of students goes on elsewhere. As with so many middle-aged men who eat too much, the lines between big and fat, between authoritative and tyrannical, blur after a while. In his quest for academic excellence, Silber has only brought to light the tendencies of most university administrators, the prejudices of most academic institutions, and the character of most academics.

4. Social Activities

As long as administrators like President Silber are being blamed for everything—including some of the economic and intellectual problems they've been hired to solve—they might as well be taken to task for the increase in sexual affairs between students and teachers. According to a recent survey, one of out of every four women receiving her Ph.D. in psychology within the last six years has slept with her professor. Given that the survey was conducted in California and that the student/teacher ratio in graduate psychology schools is less than in those of many other departments, it may be safe to assume that sevety-five percent of our nation's college students *aren't* fucking their teachers. Nevertheless, sixteen percent of the women surveyed reported sexual contact as students, eight percent as teachers, and three percent as therapists. Among the men interviewed, five percent said they had sexual contact as students, nineteen percent as teachers, and twelve percent as therapists. The only other widely known survey on this subject reports twenty-five percent of all the teachers on California State University campus admitting they had sexual relations with students.

Why? And how can tough administrators like John Silber be blamed? Let's look at it from the teachers' point of view first. Education for many people can be a very humiliating experience, not only because the more you learn the less you realize you know but also because your best efforts from the day you enter college until you defend your dissertation are constantly being criticized. Papers, exams, comprehensives, orals, the dissertation and its defense, it all adds up. And then, when you finally get to join the big Ph.D. club that you've been dreaming about for years, you find yourself on the bottom rung of another very long ladder. One with no security, a lot of work, and very little remuneration.

But there is one group who appreciates you—your students. They know nothing of the fears and anxiety you wrestled with the night before your orals, the time you got caught "borrowing" from another scholar, the poverty you may have known, the number of times your dissertation proposal was rejected, what you put your wife through while she worked to put you through school, or any of the nasty comments your professors made about your lack of preparedness, inability to conduct research, or illiterate sentence structures. All they know is you have a lot of degrees and they don't even have one. You are the *doctor*, the person you know yourself to really be, the one whose fears and anxieties are behind him—if they ever really existed—the one who commands his material dazzlingly, the one who presents it forcefully, and yes, even (dare I say it?) charmingly.

Outside the classroom, people like Silber are trying to make your life a wreck. They're telling you you've got to score high on your students' evaluations, turn your dissertation into a book, publish articles in respected journals, and serve on as many committees as you're assigned, while at the same time teach the maximum number of courses with the maximum number of students and keep plenty of office hours in case anyone wants to get in touch with you. Add to this the insecurity and distraction caused by letters that make reappointment dependent on certain budget developments, the news that the philosophy department's only woman was denied tenure in spite of the unanimous approval of her colleagues, and your superiors' advice to keep your opinions to yourself and you can see how the classroom can become a haven for peace, autonomy, and ego-massaging, which is most effective when the good-looking students do it.

There may be as many as five or even fifteen of them. Not that you plan to sleep with them *all*, just the one or two or three that give you the all-important green light. And why not? You're in the same field after all—even if at opposite ends of it—and that field provides you with common interests, things your wife no longer appreciates, like the books you've assigned for the course and the amusing interpretations and anecdotes you tell in class.

And what about the students? What's in it for them? A lot—at least at first—like learning there's an attractive person behind their work, getting a higher grade, feeling singled out as special, having the opportunity to learn more, experiencing the intrigue and excitement of an "underground" relationship, discovering how a little sexual stimulation can bring out your best efforts in class and on papers, learning the advantage of having someone who can provide you with enthusiastic recommendations and access to scholarships or stipends, and enjoying the confidence that comes from a superior's belief and interest in you, not to mention the answer to the question you've been asking all along: "What would it be like if . . . ?"

Remembering her tryst with a fifty-one-year-old professor, one student told the *Boston Globe*'s Mopsy Strange Kennedy: "He was a free thinker, and he was able to stimulate us to think critically. He would get us so excited in class that he would hop around the window-sills. I was one of his favorites and, all the time that I was formulating something interesting and provocative to say about Jane Austen, I was having wild sexual fantasies about him." The fact that he had a reputation as a controversial teacher made him even more attractive. "It made him seem like someone who would break the rules."

One day, after class, he asked her to go with him for a ride. "It was a beautiful spring day. As we drove around, I flirted outrageously with him, as I had done all year, only much more so. I got closer and closer to him, I pushed my skirt up, and I helped him light a cigarette just so I could touch him, until we finally drove off the road and made love. He had come prepared with condoms in the glove compartment, which amused and somewhat relieved me because I thought I was the one initiating all this."

Unfortunately, most professors are usually better in the classroom than they are in the back seat. "As a teacher," explains one flirter, "he seemed a lot more playful than his age would suggest. But as a lover, he suddenly seemed a lot older. His patter when he made love was embarrassing. He seemed klutzy to me."

And klutzy love-making can often only be the beginning. One student, who spent a year in a well-known creative writing program and dated an important poet there, found herself trapped in a teacher-to-student relationship. "This man acted downright superior," she said later, "especially when we were out with his friends; notice I say '*his* friends'—it would have been too degrading to meet mine. He would use the relationship to lecture me and mold my opinion of other poets."

Even a supportive relationship can be restrictive, however, because no matter which way you cut it, the student is never equal. "I was forever looking up to him and bending my knee to his greater sophistication and knowledge," remembers a student whose relationship with her professor lasted five years. "Though he helped me enormously in my career and didn't condescend in any obvious way, I didn't really unfurl my wings until we broke up. Then I finally felt I had come into my own, and I wrote two books in a fever of hard work that year."

And then there's the matter of grades. Few students enter a relationship with them in mind, but they nearly always become a factor. Although the slightest undercurrent of sexual interest can frequently stimulate a student's academic achievement, any direct sexual involvement usually disrupts the student-teacher relationship, especially in terms of the professor's objectivity. More often than not, a teacher will just give the student an "A" on the grounds that she is one of his better students, has worked hard to please him, and he believes she's probably learned more than anyone else just from being around *him*. On the other hand, there are some professors who become as tough on their lovers' work as they've been easy on their own sexual drives, and cases have been recorded of students who don't hand in any work once an affair is initiated. They have their pride too, after all, and besides, what's the teacher going to do about it? Flunk her and risk her running to the dean?

And what about the "other woman" in the professor's life? The one who worked so he could go to school, who held him in her arms the night before his orals and told him not to worry, and who now feels it's her turn to pursue a career. Well, to put it bluntly, she's become something of a drag. Now that he's found his place in the world and is a little more sure of himself, she no longer seems as interested in him. It's almost as if his anxiety and ambition have taken a toll on her regard for him. Knowing the side of him that broke down when he failed his comprehensives the first time around, she can't see him in the same light as his students, and what's worse is he can't be with her very long without remembering that terrible period in his life when he had such a poor self-image. He becomes negative and resentful towards her. He can't understand why, when he's ready to spread his wings, she still wants to mother him. Of course he feels guilty about his affair with Cheri, but he can't let a little thing like that stand in the way of his perfectly natural wish to be adored.

Which leads us to an important difference between what it means to be a faculty wife and the wife, say, of a grocer or a mailman. A mailman's wife can understand the social value of her husband's work and knows, if called upon, she could do it too; the women who bond with scholars and scientists, however, find themselves in the service of people who feel entitled to demand sacrifice from their wives without hearing any complaints because what these men are doing is not done in their own names (ho-ho) but in the name of something which transcends them all: *E*ducation, *L*aw, *H*ealth, *W*hatever. A good faculty wife understands this, finds comfort in the misery of other faculty wives, and is rewarded for her sacrifices with an acknowledgment or dedication in one of her husband's books.

Many women couldn't dream of anything that would make them happier, but what about the intelligent woman who married someone whose mind made him winning company and who followed him to his new job in the hope of finding work in the vicinity? Not much of a problem, perhaps, in New York, Chicago, or San Francisco, but what about Radford, Pueblo, or Green Bay? Rarely will she find anything to match his working conditions, rarely will she find anything at all. And when she does, it will probably be only half-time and half-hearted, which means since her husband works full-time and his job is more important, the woman must be responsible for everything else, which might not be all that much except for the fact that some tasks are energizing and some are enervating. Running to ask a colleague his opinion of a paragraph you've just written is energizing; remembering to pick up bread on your way home from the laundromat is not. Now while it is true that more and more men are accepting more and more domestic responsibilities, they can usually choose *when* they want to help; a woman often can't. Which doesn't mean her book on the Golden Age Eclogues won't get written, just that it will take a while longer. And the longer it takes, the more resentful she becomes. Slowly, almost imperceptibly at first, her husband drifts farther away from her and closer to his interested and not yet embittered students.

5. Three Case Histories

Generally speaking, a professor's tenure, promotion, and merit raises depend upon his performances in three areas: Teaching, publication, and service to the college. The key to success in most universities, however, is not achievement but a sort of well-liked mediocrity. In other words, something must be accomplished in each of these areas but never more than might be threatening to the department's tenured members: Scores just below theirs on your students' teaching evaluations, not quite as many publications and not ever in a more respected journal than the tenured Golden Boys, and lip-sealed service only on the committees to which you are assigned, which, if you show any promise at all, will be the least interesting and powerful. The particular level of achievement you can reach for, of course, is determined by the strength of the department. The better the department, the higher you can set your goals.

Of the three criteria for staying in any single department, service to the college is the least important. As long as you attend the committee meetings you are assigned to and don't make waves, you will get the credit you need for tenure or promotion. To try to impress your colleagues by being more responsible, not settling for less, or creating any contributions of your own, however, is sure to invite reprisal. I know of one professor who tried to excel in this field by making whatever contributions she could wherever she saw a need. Because she had taught in a wide range of high schools and colleges, she had learned a lot about solving different kinds of problems. The professors she worked with, however, were mostly in their late fifties, had gotten tenure early in their careers when all they had to do was be liked, had never taught anywhere else, and weren't interested in having their good life interrupted by anything approaching work—a common situation in colleges that have established a Floating Bottom or large adjunct pool. The young professor's job, as they saw it, was to keep her mouth shut, record the minutes of the meetings, and write up any proposals that the committee might want the faculty-at-large to consider. There was little danger of this happening, however; not one of the four committees she served on had been able to formulate a single proposal on their assigned tasks in over three years.

So this new professor wrote the minutes and looked for ways to make her own contributions to the college. She didn't have to look far. Because she believed in breaking down the conventional barriers that tend to alienate people from one another, she asked her students to call her by her first name. She wanted to earn their respect, not take it as a given because of her position. To get to know them further, she organized and played on several intramural sports teams that she formed with the students in her classes. She also initiated a series of student-faculty games, which because of the rules she laid out beforehand, didn't revert to the opportunities for revenge she had seen in so many high school contests.

Not one to limit her resources to the classroom and the gym, she was the first professor in the history of the university to bring her students to its famous special collections library. Through the assignments given in her interdisciplinary humanities classes, her students got to read and work with, among other things, Martin Luther King, Jr.'s hate mail and various "solutions" to the Jewish problem proposed by the

Nazi medical profession. There was even time to flip through fifty-five of Bette Davis' scrapbooks and try on a mask from *Planet of the Apes.*

The curator of the library appreciated the young professor's interest and support and asked her if there was any way the other students and teachers in her college could be exposed to the wonders of the special collections library. The professor knew of a glass exhibition case in the school lobby that was filled with souvenirs a retired professor had brought back with him from vacations in Europe and the Middle East—everything from a six-inch-high model of Michelangelo's David to a six-inch-wide model of the painted tambourines that accompany the Tarantella. In fact, six inches seemed to be the standard measurement of everything in the case, a reflection, no doubt, of the collector's travel bag.

The dean of the college was delighted. He had been trying for years to think of something to do with the junk in that case. Officially, it was called a "museum," but everyone knew it as Myron's "tchatchke shelf." An agreement was made between the college and the library to have a new exhibition placed in the case every semester with a collection of World War I posters to be the opening show. The museum's "curator," however, wouldn't hear of it. He had been dusting those shelves for years, and he was not about to see its riches replaced by anything so limited in range and scope as World War I posters.

And that was the end of it. The dean wasn't about to step on the toes of someone whose support he might someday need just because the special collections library wanted to drum up a little business and, as for the students missing out on anything the library had to offer, well, what they didn't know wouldn't hurt them. The new professor, on the other hand, had just made her first real enemy.

At the time, it didn't seem important. There were so many other things to do. Like arranging theatre parties for her students and receptions afterwards where they got to meet people like Elizabeth Sados and Edward Albee. And then there was the Christmas trip to New York to meet the writers of some of the books they had read and see the King Tut exhibit, followed by the spring trip to Europe, where the students in her art history course would visit Venice, Florence, and Rome.

She didn't have a chance. Instead of recognizing what she brought to the college and made possible for her students, the tenured professors thought she was making them look bad. She had more energy than all of them put together. Rather than make additional use of that energy or think about ways to improve their own acts, however, the senior faculty got rid of her before it became too hard to get rid of her, and, it must be admitted, the untenured teachers felt better after their major competitor was gone.

* * *

The second most important criterion, but still not very important, for judging a professor's worth is his teaching ability. The first source of this measurement is the students' evaluations. Though they usually contain less than a dozen questions like:

> Did you find the reading assignments helpful?
>
> Did the instructor let you know about your progress either by grades, comments, or personal discussion?
>
> and Did the homework assignments help you to learn the course material?

Most administrators don't even bother to look at the students' evaluations. They know the teachers don't allow any questions that they haven't already approved. You'd have to be a moron not to do well. For example, how could a reading assignment *not* be helpful? How could a student go through a whole course and *not* receive a grade or comment? How could a homework assignment *not* help someone learn? I know a teacher who has literally never shown up on time, always ended his class early, never corrected more than half the papers he assigned, always taken off the maximum days allowed, and never failed anybody who at least showed up for class *or* handed in most of his assignments. He's one of the most popular teachers in his college.

There are some schools, on the other hand, where teaching is said to be important. These are usually community colleges, however, or programs within a larger university. In these programs, the students' evaluation forms may be more extensive. Although the questions have still been subjected to the faculty's approval, there may be as many as twenty-four of them:

> Do you think the instructor is objective in his evaluation of a student's performance?
>
> Does the instructor come to class prepared?
>
> Is the instructor's course material well organized?
>
> Is the instructor's material presented in an interesting manner?
>
> Does the instructor generate enthusiasm for his subject matter?

These are stickier questions to be sure, especially if the results are open to interpretation. A friend of mine, who was just beginning her teaching career, once asked me if I had any advice to offer. I told her about Mrs. Goldburg's beginning every class with a ten-minute, five-question, short-answer quiz. Even though Mrs. Goldburg's students were in high school, I didn't think my friend's students were all that different. Both groups needed to develop a sense of discipline.

What happened was easy to predict. The students objected at first but soon came to see the quizzes as more of a help than a hindrance. True, they had to prepare for them and attend every class (there were no make-ups), but they were also learning to enjoy the reading they had rarely done in high school. They saw themselves improving as they became accustomed to answering my friend's questions, and as the good grades piled up, they gained confidence in their ability to understand and then explain what they had read. Their writing improved; their comprehension improved; even their retention improved. When the final grades were posted, my friend's students were among the highest in the college.

But my friend wasn't content with getting her students to be responsible; she wanted to channel their energy into other areas as well. So she taught them how to conduct research and lead their own discussions. I was invited to the class and was impressed by how the students could lead themselves into learning experiences that were well beyond anything I thought them capable of. Incorporating my friend's ideas into my own courses, I learned as well from the research they conducted and the variety of approaches they came up with to satisfy their own interests.

Phi Delta Kappan, a magazine for teachers, published an article on our findings, and the students showed their appreciation by giving my friend almost astronomical marks on their evaluations. On a scale of 1 to 5 with 5 being the highest mark a teacher could receive in each of twenty categories, my friend's scores averaged 4.71, 4.74, and 4.77 in each of the three years she taught, and twice she was nominated to receive the university's highest teaching award, an honor usually reserved for tenured professors who have been at the school for ten years or more.

Her success was short-lived, however. There were a few murmurs her first year when the other professors on her teaching team wondered if the quizzes were making the students concentrate more on literature and neglect their other subjects. As my friend moved form one teaching team to another, the murmurs grew louder. Several professors refused to work with her. The shit didn't really hit the fan, however, until some of her ex-students began showing up their sophomore-year professors. Having learned to conduct research in my friend's class, they began parroting in front of others the same information their teachers had researched. My friend was accused of undermining the authority of her colleagues. Her department chairman called her quizzes "unscrupulous" and "immoral." He said her students' high grades were not an indication of their achievement but rather the means by which she had manipulated them into giving her the highest evaluations in the college.

Fortunately, the dean knew better and pointed out that the

four professors who gave higher grades to their students all received lower marks on their evaluations, two of which were among the very lowest in the college. That's because they're good teachers, my friend's enemies replied. They make their students work for those grades; that's why their evaluations are so low.

My friend saw what she was up against: the evaluations could be interpretated anyway anyone wanted. What mattered was not how well you taught but how well you were liked. She had threatened the mediocrity of the status quo and now she was going to pay for it. Generously, the dean gave her one year to find another job.

* * *

Regardless of much evidence to the contrary, publication is still considered to be the most important criterion for determining promotion, tenure, and merit, and the pressure to publish—anything, anywhere—is enormous. So enormous, in fact, that junior professors have become prime victims for financially troubled publishers. And what beginning professor is going to jeopardize his chances for tenure, damage the reputation of his work, and risk the moral suspicion of his colleagues to expose Project Innovation of California or New York University Press? It's easier to pay the money, get the credit, and forget about it. Unfortunately, the levels to which a desperate scholar can sink are not limited to paying publication costs.

The most successfully published junior professor I've ever known was a fellow student in graduate school. How he ever got admitted to a doctoral program was beyond just about everybody in our class. Behind his back, people used to say he was the only Ph.D. candidate in the country who didn't know the names "Henry" and "James" went together. What was even more amazing was that he didn't care if he didn't know anything. He wasn't ashamed that he ranked at the bottom of his class in every course he took, nor that he was the only student ever to take his comprehensive exams without satisfying the university's minimal requirement of at least one "A" in over fifty-four credit hours worth of courses.

Something happened to him, however, when he began studying for his comprehensives. Suddenly, he turned serious. Every day for seven months, he devoted at least twelve hours to making up for all he hadn't read. Some days, he didn't even sleep. In one weekend, he knocked off James Joyce's *Portrait of the Artist as a Young Man*, Virginia Woolf's *To the Lighthouse*, Ernest hemingway's *The Sun Also Rises*, and D.H. Lawrence's *The Rainbow* plus a major part of the criticism. Of the scores of students sitting for the comprehensives—a twelve-hour exam written over three days—he was one of only a handful to pass with distinction in all six categories.

Some people bloom late; this guy exploded. Among other things that year, he sang with a chorus in Carnegie Hall and finished 1,007th in the New York Marathon. His dissertation proposal was on Samuel Beckett, which was something of a coup for him because he had written to Beckett and the world's greatest living writer had invited him to Paris—an opportunity most scholars would kill for. When he returned from Paris, this once part-time student/full-time clown had a proposal that was going to knock everybody's socks off. Or at least roll them down a bit.

Every single member of the graduate faculty rejected it, one of them noting: "Sounds like this boy's been talking to Beckett." He meant it as a negative comment on the student's esoteric topic, which had something to do with every success being a failure, but my friend took it as a compliment.

Taking rejection as a compliment didn't help him write a more acceptable proposal, however. In fact, everything he submitted was rejected. Then he realized why. His reputation was written on the title page of every proposal he wrote. No one would accept his proposals because no one wanted to work with him. Professors began leaving him outside their offices for hours and, when he wouldn't go away and they couldn't stay any longer, they'd tell him to come back the next day. No one would make an appointment with him.

So the student had to find a professor who didn't know who he was. Finally, he found one, but there was a problem. The student's interest was in literature; the only professor who didn't know him taught linguistics. Fortunately for the student, the professor seemed to like him. He asked the student whom he would write about if he could write about anyone in the world. The student told him: William Goldman.

William Goldman. A twentieth-century American novelist, who is known mostly for his screenplays: *Butch Cassidy and the Sundance Kid*, *All the President's Men*, *Marathon Man*, and at least a half dozen more. All blockbusters. Goldman is Hollywood's highest paid, most successful screenwriter, but this kid wanted to write about his novels. Why? Because Goldman's books were the only ones he had read in high school and college that weren't assigned in class.

Fair enough, but no one in the English Department had ever read a book by Goldman. No one could advise a dissertation on *The Temple of Gold* or *Boys and Girls Together* or *The Princess Bride* if he or she wanted to, and no one, absolutely no one, was going to read twelve novels by anybody he or she didn't know.

Except the linguistics professor. He hadn't read anything by Goldman either, but that was the reason he decided to do it. He thought he might learn something.

So a deal was worked out. A professor in American literature would be the official advisor, but it was the linguistics professor who would make sure the dissertation was written properly. This pleased everybody. The student could write his dissertation, and no one in literature would have to read it. There was some resistance to Goldman's worth as a subject, but, as the official advisor pointed out, he was a perfect writer for the candidate. Goldman wasn't Henry James, but the student wasn't Leon Edel either. And if the student could meet Goldman, he'd possibly get an interview and access to manuscripts that would provide him with a "scholarly experience" even if it wasn't a very rich one.

Goldman was surprised that someone in academia had finally shown an interest in his books. "When I die," he told the student, "I don't want somebody writing 'Screenwriter' on my tombstone. Whatever I am, if it's of any interest at all, it's in those novels." Goldman also said something which would have a profound effect on the student: "The difference between me and the greatest writer that's ever lived and the worst writer you can think of is not all that great. What we all have in common is the ability to go into a room, shut the door, and not come out until the book is done."

That writing a book could depend more on discipline than talent was something the student had never thought of. Could he write a book too? He knew from the way he studied for his comprehensives that he had the discipline.

When the dissertation was finished and his oral defense passed—Beckett would have appreciated the absurdity of five professors grilling a person for two hours on twelve books they hadn't read—the student accepted a teaching position at a mediocre university in the great Mid-Waste.

Over the first summer vacation, he turned his dissertation into a book and wrote his first novel, a story about the ways students and teachers can abuse each other. The following fall he learned the realities of publishing. New York University Press told him they'd print his book on William Goldman *if* he included his interviews with the author in an appendum, *if* he found someone like Robert Redford or Dustin Hoffman to write the introduction, and *if* he came up with $2,000 to "subvent" the publishing costs. Where did N.Y.U. Press think he was going to get $2,000? That was more than one-sixth of his salary. An editor suggested tapping Goldman—a man who thinks writing jacket blurbs is whoring—for the money. If John Updike could give the press $2,000 for a book on his works, why couldn't Goldman? He was a millionaire after all he could afford it. Besides, he needed the book if he wanted to be considered a serious writer.

Friends of the new professor told him paying off publishers was a standard practice, made a lot cheaper if he could submit a copy produced on a word processor. One friend had received a $4,000 grant from his university to pay for the publication of a book, had his work produced on a word processor, found a publisher who would print the book for less than $2,000, and used the rest of the money for a well-deserved vacation in the Bahamas. The new professor, who thought this was terrible, wrote an article about what was going on and sent it off to Project Innovation, which agreed to publish his "timely and important" piece in an upcoming issue of their magazine for $128.

Selling the novel was a different matter. The publisher didn't ask him for any money, but my friend wondered if they would have if *60 Minutes* had not done a segment on their charging some poor woman $10,000 to print a book about her toy poodle. What they did do to him, however, may have been worse. The book, which included homosexual abuse among the many ways teachers and students exploit each other, was marketed as a gay novel, and the professor unexpectedly found himself scheduled to appear on a number of radio and television shows during Gay Pride Week.

Just about the time his novel became a Lambda Book Club Selection, *William Goldman* was accepted for publication in Twayne Press's United States Authors Series. The book was so successful that the professor was asked to write one on Robert Coover, which, when it was published, Jerome Klinkowitz called "one of the finest contributions to innovative fiction scholarship."

Our professor was on his way. Out. That his colleagues couldn't come to grips with the novel is understandable. In addition to its packaging, they weren't familiar with the fabulist tradition in which it was written and criticized it for all the reasons that made it fabulist—the emphasis on construction, the wide range of narrative techniques, the multiple voices, the juxtaposition of the fantastic and everyday, and the pasteboard effect of its paragraphs, which gave them the impression they could all be scooped up, reshuffled, and laid down again without altering the book's major elements.

William Goldman put them on a more sure footing, but they questioned whether this novelist-turned-screenwriter was worthy of serious consideration. In their eyes, the book became a symbol of what happens to a publishing company when it is taken over by International Telephone and Telegraph. Twayne was cranking out books like Hostess, another ITT subsidiary, was producing cupcakes. The critical study of Robert Coover's fictions confirmed this theory, and when our new professor mentioned Klinkowitz's appraisal, his chairman replied, "Jerome who?"

What these books really symbolized, however, was the chairman's own shortcomings. Within two years, this new professor, this decidedly "unprofessional turk from New York," had outpublished the combined career efforts of his entire department. And where he would end was anybody's guess. Possibly in the chairman's own chair. The dean had already given him the largest percentage salary increase in the college, and an agent from Hollywood had telephoned to talk about buying the screenplay rights to his second novel. What *second* novel? The chairman didn't know anything about any *second* novel.

But the new professor did. The *New York Times Book Review* had called his recent fictional history about a tribe of Indians "a human story, passionately told," and Hubert Selby, Jr. thought it was a "work of art, not ego." The chairman, however, knew better. "To write a book like that," he told the professor, "takes absolutely no talent whatsoever." That the chairman hadn't read the book didn't matter; he knew mediocrity when he saw it.

* * *

So there you have them. The rules of the game. Make fireworks in the classroom if you wish, but make sure they don't show up on your students' evaluations. Organize field trips if you want, but don't make anyone look as if he's not doing his job. Publish if you must, but don't outdo the highest ranking members of your department or you *will* perish.

And there you have the results. Three outstanding individuals, each capable of making an important contribution to whatever school they're in, pushed from one Floating Bottom to another until they learn not to think, not question, not to create, and not to try to change the way things are. What is perhaps most unusual about these people, however, is that they're not three separate persons. They're all one and the same, a currently underemployed adjunct who, though not yet among the nationally renowned, threatens an awful lot of people at that level. And he's not alone either. There are hundreds like him all across the country: young, talented, ambitious scholars who find in their work the satisfaction denied them by threatened superiors and administrators whose reluctance to rock the boat is helping to sink the ship.

V

The Tip of the Iceberg

Having relinquished their authority over what determines a college education and caved in almost completely to marketing considerations, America's universities are failing to give their students an understanding of the culture and civilization they are preparing to enter. The result is a generation of trained specialists whose lives outside of their workplace are often stilted and pedestrian. It may be good for the economy, but is it good for society?

Conventional wisdom blames the near abandonment of the humanities—that special body of literature, philosophy, history, and art from which our highest values were formed—on the demand for high paying jobs, but academia's failure to demonstrate and insist on their importance is also responsible. By increasing the range of vocational courses, relegating the required humanities classes to the first years of study, and hiring so many unqualified, inexperienced, and uncommitted adjuncts to teach them, university administrators have given today's students a shortsighted and shortchanged view of what knowledge matters most.

Nor has our civilization received much help from its professors. Whereas historians and literature specialists used to be responsible for the more sweeping survey courses, they now insist on classes which correspond more closely to their own narrow interests. And on the few occasions when they're obligated to teach a survey course, they frequently rely on dated books, tired notes, and recycled exams. Similarly, foreign language specialists who see language instruction as a waste of their time and talent quickly establish reputations for classes that are mechanical, unchallenging, and dull.

As a result of this decline in humanistic interests, today's students can earn bachelors' degrees from seventy-five percent of all American colleges and universities without having studied European history, from seventy-two percent without having taken a course in American literature, and from eighty-six percent without knowing anything about the civilizations of classical Greece and Rome. In 1966, ninety percent of our colleges required foreign language study for graduation; today only forty-seven percent do. Deprived of their culture's highest ideals, lasting visions, and shared heritage, today's students lack a body of knowledge and means of inquiry for discovering and conveying serious truths about the perennial questions of life that our civilization's greatest works address.

The first appointed professors of humanities served at Oxford College early in the sixteenth century. Their job was to conserve the learning and tradition of classical Greece and Rome, but what they learned and taught others was so relevant to the human experience, it became the foundation upon which the idea of a liberal education was built.

With the proliferation and fragmentation of knowledge initiated by Newton and the increased reliance on technology since the eighteenth century, however, the humanities have sought refuge in their colleges' ivy towers and bolted the doors. Rather than participate in the world's exciting and sometimes frightening developments, they've reinforced their role as conservers at the expense of imagination and innovation. When Thoreau wanted to study his favorite writer, Shakespeare, for example, he was told Harvard didn't offer any courses in the moderns.

A similar situation exists today. While the world moves forward at ever increasing speeds, those who profess the humanities remain in their towers guarding our heritage and disseminating its insights and values to fewer and fewer students. These values must be liberated, however, if they are to continue to play an active role in shaping our civilization. They must be injected back into life's mainstream in terms that apply to the social, political, and economic realities of our age. In other words, they must once again *humanize*.

And they better begin soon. We live in a world of increasing insensitivity. Terrorism may be the first example to come to many minds, but the process is much deeper and farther ranging. A kind of cultural numbing is taking place in this country that is undermining our human spirit and reducing us to passive, dehumanized machines. What Emerson would call MEN NON-THINKING.

Let me give you an example of what I mean. In the fall of 1985, the *Columbus* (Ohio) *Dispatch*, as average a newspaper as you could hope to find, ran a multipart series on prostitution. The stories went on for at least five days, but three people stuck in my memory: A man who had AIDS but thought nothing of giving it to others, a girl who had been arrested 100 times before her 18th birthday, and a 10-year-old boy who gives blow jobs on his way home from school.

These are shocking identities, but that was all the reporter told us about them.

Whatever happened in the life of the man who had AIDS that led him to spread his terrible disease without a twinge of guilt?

What kind of family does a girl with 100 arrests before she's 18 come from?

And how does a kid in the third grade even hear about blow jobs, let alone learn how to give one?

We never knew, and the reason we never knew was the reporter never saw these people as people. He saw them as problems or issues to be dealt with and so did his readers. When the series ended and all the letters to the editor were in, the Columbus police chief announced he was assigning six more officers to patrol the area in which the prostitutes hung out.

Reporters, readers, police chief—they all missed half the story and, as a result, responded in the only way they knew how! Which another flood of letters applauded.

But what about the prostitutes? Did throwing them in jail for the night or driving them to other street corners solve Columbus's problem?

The answer is obvious. Had the reporter focused as much on the subjective world of these people as he had on their objective one, a more humane or understanding or compassionate or even fruitful solution might have been reached.

Unfortunately, journalists are not trained to look at the world in human terms. As a result, we read daily about murder, rape, and rising utility rates but very little about love, hate, anxiety, guilt, or stress. We read about people's external worlds but precious little about the internal worlds these external worlds reflect. We read about experiences without ever discovering the nature of these experiences.

And this way of looking at the world is not limited to journalists. I recently spoke to a group of teachers about the ways educators teach children to distance themselves from their feelings, and the talk drifted to our use of euphemisms and the unconscious effects they may have on children over a long period of time.

The teachers seemed to agree with much of what I had to say until I brought up corporal punishment as an example. By referring to paddling as corporal punishment and talking about it as a means of maintaining control in the classroom, teachers in the 42 states where hitting students is legal never have to think of themselves as child abusers.

In Columbus in one recent year there were over 30,000 registered beatings, but not one of the Central Ohioans I spoke with would admit that any child had been hit. They may have been paddled with boards but they had never been hit and, as one teacher put it, it wasn't the paddling that was so important in correcting a student's behavior as the humiliation he suffered in front of his classmates.

Sharing the insensitivity platform with teachers and journalists are many of our nation's political leaders. Do we listen to the message behind the detached, objective, almost inhuman ways our government's spokespeople talk about the United Nations, the World Court, Nicaragua, or the nuclear accident at Chernobyl?

People in other parts of the world do. And what they hear is an increase in American insensitivity. Typical of the dozens of "American" jokes currently making the rounds in Europe these days is one about an insurance salesman who comes home from work to find his house blown apart by terrorists and his family in body-bags all over the front lawn. A group

MANNING THE PUMPS

of reporters rush to ask him how he feels. The man stiffens, a detached glaze comes over his eyes, and then he says something that sounds as though it came right out of the mouth of Robby the Robot.

After the Space Challenger exploded all over our television screens, people in England noted that when someone died in America he wasn't really dead, only suffering "a possible major malfunction."

Now it's one thing to think this way. And it's another to talk this way. But what about when we begin acting this way? What happens when our substance begins imitating our style?

Unfortunately, it has been for some time.

Remember the Ford Pinto? Remember how it could explode if another car hit it in the rear? Did you know that the Ford Motor Company knew those cars might explode but decided not to install a safety device because it was cheaper to let people die?

Here's how Ford came to this conclusion. Before putting the Pinto on the market, Ford engineers tested and recommended three devices that would prevent the Pinto's gas tank from rupturing in a rear-end collision. One device cost $1, another cost around $5, and the third cost $11.

Ford compared the cost of implementing each safety device with the number of cars it planned to produce. Using statistics compiled by the National Highway Traffic Safety Administration, Ford estimated that without the $11 safety feature, 2,100 cars would burn every year, 180 people would burn to death, and another 180 would survive serious injury. Ford then estimated that each survivor's medical bills would cost them $67,000, each death $200,000, and each Pinto $700. Given the market—11 million cars and 1.5 million trucks—the company concluded that the money it could save by building a better car ($49.5 million) wasn't worth the money it would spend on a safety device ($137.5 million). Neither, apparently, were the 500 people who burned to death in Pinto crashes between 1971 and 1977.

It is unlikely that journalists, central Ohioan school teachers, and moralists at the Ford Motor Company can do anything to reverse this trend and change our image abroad.

But the people who run our colleges and universities, the people who decide what our future journalists, teachers, and engineers study, can begin the process of humanizing our culture by introducing a revitalized humanities program to a central place in the college curriculum. To achieve this, today's students must learn to appreciate the practical advantages of a liberal education. They must see—at least to get them started—that there's money in it. They must discover that liberal arts graduates are able to communicate more effectively with a wider spectrum of peers, subordinates and managers. They must realize that thinking analytically serves them in banking as well as in history.

Fortunately, this shouldn't be a difficult lesson to grasp. Recent studies indicate that humanities majors have a greater potential for management than business or engineering majors and, of the four hundred corporate executives interviewed by the American Telephone and Telegraph Company in 1983, eighty percent of them rated communication skills and reasoning ability as crucial to success in business. And with the jobs most people are going to hold in ten years not yet created, there's going to be an increased need for people with the kinds of flexible minds and adaptable skills that accounting, marketing, and economics won't provide but a strong liberal arts program can.

Bradford College in Massachusetts is among the leaders in the fight to provide a practical liberal arts education. Begun in 1983, Bradford's program requires its students to declare an interdisciplinary major, such as creative arts or human studies, and a career-oriented minor, such as public relations or technical writing. The students are also required to participate in a range of general education courses ranging from ethics to alienation as well as complete a one-term paid internship.

To demonstrate the worth of such a program, Bradford's president, Arthur Levine, cites a study that says the average liberal arts major rises higher on the corporate ladder than the average business major. The reason for this, he claims, is that the issues of work are life issues which are best covered in a humanities curriculum. And somebody must be listening to him. Bradford has received twenty-five percent more applications since its program was put into effect.

For schools that are too big to establish the kind of interdisciplinary program offered at Bradford, a recent report by the National Endowment for the Humanities suggests a core of common studies that includes a chronological understanding of the development of Western civilization, a careful reading of selected masterworks in English, American, and European literature, an understanding of the most significant philosophical ideas, familiarity with at least one non-Western culture, and demonstrable proficiency in a foreign language.

The importance of learning a foreign language and the exposure it affords to the culture of another nation cannot be overemphasized. Few barriers to the increased interdependence with other nations have been as formidable as those raised by the parochialism of America's educators. By allowing the foreign language requirements to be waived in over half our country's colleges, administrators have encouraged the kind of isolationist thinking that's undermined the nation's performance in international trade, underestimated the competition that's reached our shores from abroad, and severely impaired our foreign policy strategies.

To help reverse this trend, Wheaton College in Massachusetts, with a grant from the Exxon Education Foundation, has begun a program to expose its teachers firsthand to the cultures of other nations in the hope that they will incorporate what they learn into their own course. So far, the program's success has been qualified only by the short lengths of stay in the foreign countries. Few of the professors had the time to develop long-lasting friendships, and others worried that their views may be shallow or distorted. Nevertheless, professors in various disciplines have been able to incorporate Buddhist teachings into their behavioral psychology classes and produce an anthology of English-language Kenyan poetry. Broader objectives for the program include visits by foreign dignitaries, extending the program to other colleges, encouraging personal faculty projects, and improving the local industry by using the new found knowledge of other cultures to educate its executives. The program is also of benefit to any students from a country one of their professors may have visited. "When you know a teacher has gone to your country you can develop a special bond," claims a student from the Phillippines. "They seem to have touched your life. They really understand."

Your college doesn't have to wait for a grant from Exxon, however, to introduce the influences of a foreign culture to your campus. Many of the same effects that Wheaton is experiencing can be produced simply by hiring one of the scores of underemployed former Fulbright scholars or professors. Just getting someone from another part of the country would help many departments. I recently took a group of students from Atlanta on a tour of New York, and when it was over, their professor told me: "I really appreciate your showing the kids around the way you did. Coming from the South, it's good for them to meet someone who's Jewish from New York."

Practical liberal arts programs ... common cores of humanities courses ... foreign travel—it all sounds pretty exciting, but none of it will happen if the best possible teachers aren't hired or developed and humanists don't successfully bridge the gap between themselves and the scientists and businessmen they've traditionally scorned.

I met recently with a humanities professor from one of those Harvard-of-the-West universities. He had taken a dozen of his students to New York for a week and was asked by his chairman to interview me for a position I had applied for in their department. My impression of the humanities professor was that he was warm, personable, and had a genuine interest in and affection for his students, but his knowledge of the humanities was shockingly limited to literature. On a trip to the Frick Collection, for example, he told his students that Holbein was a master of light and pointed out how it shone on Thomas More's face while all below was dark, that Thomas Cromwell overthrew England's monarchical government, and that Gainsborough had painted perfectly, (from his imagination,) the folds in a dress. "Gainsborough really knew where the folds were," he said. "Look at those folds." And the students dutifully looked at the dress. Standing in front of a work by Fra Lippo Lippi—"the painter made famous by Browning's poem"—he complained that Lippi didn't know anything about light because his painting doesn't tell us where to stand when we look at it.

As good a teacher as this professor may be, his breadth of knowledge does not qualify him to serve in a humanities program. Nevertheless, he's probably closer to the norm than many people might expect. When I was teaching freshman humanities at the College of Basic Studies, I was one of only two professors on that level to teach art history and music appreciation in addition to literature, and yet, when people read the other students' transcripts, they're going to see and believe those students have had a full year of humanities.

Perhaps it is a lack of general knowledge more than anything else that has encouraged those in the humanities to cling to their Western centrism, their self-proclaimed elitism, their exclusion of science, and their insistence on their own absolutism. The longer they cling, however, the farther removed from the real world will they be. And the less patient and tolerant they are with scientists and technologists, the smaller will their own audience grow.

The humanities, then, have got to take steps, however small or reluctant, toward accepting a more responsible role in the world if they want to insure their own survival.

And it's not as if they have nothing to offer. Even the most limited humanities professor can contribute a critical sensitivity, an ability to communicate, an appreciation of the past, an understanding of the present, a sense of life's range and scope, and, most importantly, an awareness of our civilization's highest values, values not as dogma to hit scientists and politicians over the head with but as milestones or guideposts for exploring and understanding the human condition within the context of today's world.

Humanists can't halt a famine in Ethiopia, but they can influence the way we think about the people there. In other words, those in the humanities must begin responding to crises in the world. As conservers of the human tradition in the finest sense of that word, they must meet the challenge of expressing its highest ideals forcefully, eloquently, and permanently. Only then will we be able to claim that we are a nation of *educated* people.